#1 INTERNATIONAL BESTSELLER

STARTUP SECRETS

FOR ENTREPRENEURS

How To Create Specific Strategies To Build Your List, Make Offers And Connect With Your Best Buyers

STARTUP SECRETS FOR ENTREPRENEURS

How To Create Specific Strategies To Build Your List, Make Offers And Connect With Your Best Buyers

By

John North

Evolvepreneur offers many ways for you to get involved and even interact with like-minded individuals and we look forward to hearing from you and especially your wins.

Grab Your Free Book Bonus: *https://startupsecretsbook.com/page/book-bonus*

Here are a few ways to connect with us:
- Join our free Facebook Group
- Listen to our Podcast
- Download our Mobile App
- Join as a regular or mastermind member
- Become one of our experts and help our community

All of this can be found at *www.evolvepreneur.club* and we are waiting right now...

Copyright

By JOHN NORTH (c) Copyright 2020

Edited by James North

All rights reserved.

Book Layout ©2020

www.EvolveGlobalPublishing.com

No part of this book may be reproduced or transmitted in any form or by any means, electronic or mechanical, including photocopying, recording or by any information storage and retrieval system, without written permission from the authors, except for the inclusion of brief quotations in a review.

Limit of Liability Disclaimer: The information contained in this book is for information purposes only, and may not apply to your situation. The author, publisher, distributor, and provider provide no warranty about the content or accuracy of content enclosed. Information provided is subjective. Keep this in mind when reviewing this guide. Neither the Publisher nor the Author shall be liable for any loss of profit or any other commercial damages resulting from the use of this guide. All links are for information purposes only and are not warranted for content, accuracy, or any other implied or explicit purpose.

Earnings Disclaimer: All income examples in this book are just that – examples. They are not intended to represent or guarantee that everyone will achieve the same results. You understand that each individual's success will be determined by his or her desire, dedication, background, effort, and motivation to work. There is no guarantee you will duplicate any of the results stated here. You recognize any business endeavours has inherent risk or loss of capital.

Startup Secrets for Entrepreneurs

How To Create Specific Strategies To Build Your List, Make Offers And Connect With Your Best Buyers

1st Edition. 2020

ASIN: B088K64W7R (Amazon Kindle)

ISBN: 979-8-64649-997-5 (Amazon Print)

ISBN: 979-8-40884-664-1 (Amazon Hardcover)

ISBN: 978-1-63752-075-8 (Ingram Spark) PAPERBACK

ISBN: 978-1-63752-076-5 (Ingram Spark) HARDCOVER

ISBN: 9780463157688 (Smashwords)

CONTACT THE AUTHOR:

Business Name: EVOLVE SYSTEMS GROUP PTY LTD

Author Website: www.johnnorth.com.au

Main Website: www.EvolveGlobalPublishing.com

LinkedIn: https://au.linkedin.com/in/johnnorth1085

Twitter: @johnnorth7 and @evolvepreneur

Book Bonus: *https://startupsecretsbook.com/page/book-bonus*

Email: john@evolvesys.com.au

Phone: 1300 889 383

TRADEMARKS

All product names, logos, and brands are the property of their respective owners. All company, product, and service names used in this book are for identification purposes only. The use of these names, logos, and brands does not imply endorsement. All other trademarks cited herein are the property of their respective owners.

SPECIAL OFFER TO OUR READERS!

Grab our 100% Free Bonuses valued at thousands of dollars which include:

- Goal Setting Think Sheets
- 3 Part Marketing Strategies Video Series
- 10 Part Audio & Workbook Series
- Goal Setting for Life and Freedom Course
- Entrepreneurs Guide to Focus Blueprint
- Massive Motivation Course
- Entrepreneurial Success Course
- Success Habits Course
- Day pass to the Evolvepreneur Summit
- 4 Complete Sample Marketing Portfolios to Model

www.startupsecretsbook.com/page/book-bonus

Table of Contents

About The Author 9
My Entrepreneurial Journey 13
Introduction 25
Our Startup Framework 27

Part One - Mindset 29
   What is the Founder Stage? 31
   Your Primary Mission 39
   The Importance of Goal-Setting 41
   What Are Your Personal Objectives? 47
   Action Steps and Summary 49

Part Two - Strategy 51
   Developing a Strategic Objective 53
   Creating a Business Plan 59
   Launch Ideas 61
   Fast Market Research 63
   The Buyers Journey 65

Part Three - Implementation 69
   The New Online Business System 71
   Websites, Landing Pages and Sales Pages 75
   Podcasting 79
   Your Own Show 83
   Building Subscribers 87
   Memberships and Recurring Income 89
   Success Journeys 91
   Surveys for Success 93
   Courses and Masterminds 95

Good Project Management is Vital! 97
Coaching and Consulting 101
Affiliates and Referral Partners 105
Writing a Book 113
If You Can't Automate It You Can't Scale It! 121
Staff Training and Systems 127

Part Four - Measure and Review 131
What's a KPI? 133
Tracking and Monitoring Your Results 137

Part Five - Pivot and Repeat 139
Creating Your Strategic Plan 141
Why Failure is Important 143
Expanding Through Advertising 145
The Future of Social Media 151

Wrapping Up 153
Did you enjoy this book? 155
Where To From Here? 157
Working with John North 159
About Evolve Global Publishing 161
About Evolve Your Business 165
About Evolvepreneur.app 167
About Evolvepreneur.club 169
Other Books By The Author 171

About The Author

John North is a Seven-Time #1 International Best-Selling Author, He is regarded as a versatile and experienced entrepreneur with a solid background in Accounting, Banking, Business Management, Finance, Personal Development, IT, Software and Strategic Marketing.

John has written seven #1 Best-Selling books about book publishing, business strategy and internet marketing, and Squash.

John is the CEO of Evolve Systems Group. He is a serial entrepreneur who has created many products and services that are designed to empower business owners and entrepreneurs. Some of these ventures include: Evolve Global Publishing, Evolvepreneur.app, Evolvepreneur.club, EvolveYourBusiness, and Evolve Mobile.

John is passionate about helping business owners become smarter and more strategic about their marketing efforts. He constantly pushes the envelope of what's possible in this modern era and is widely regarded among his peers as very innovative and highly creative in his approach.

Evolve Global Publishing is a premium service that John created to enable him to help thousands rather than hundreds of entrepreneurs. He believes that anyone can follow a system to success, but the missing keys are implementation and accountability. The Evolve Global Publishing platform and its methodologies allow an entrepreneur and potential author to create and publish their own book in a little as 90 days without writing a single word!

His latest venture, *Evolvepreneur.app*, is an all-in-one platform designed to allow entrepreneurs to take control of their future by being less reliant on social media for managing their business online.

John lives in Sydney, Australia with his wife and son and plays competitive squash 5 days a week.

After leaving school at age 15, he started his first job as a bank employee in a small country town. Throughout the next 12 years, his roles in the bank included front office, supervision, legal, and lending. The bank taught him many skills; including management, systems, and procedures, and how to handle unhappy customers!

Along the way, he trained as an ambulance and state emergency services officer. He even received an Australia Day award for services to the local community.

In 1989, John started getting very interested in the emerging computer revolution and founded a part-time computer and accounting software business. After building and working on this new business, he soon realised the huge opportunity that was emerging in the field of technology, so he resigned from the bank and started working on his new business full-time. In just a few years, it quickly grew to over $1.5 million per year in recurring revenue.

In 2000, Australia introduced a new sales tax "GST" system, and his business went from boom to bust—the new tax drove businesses to computerise en masse for the reporting they needed to do, which sucked all new revenue from future years. The computer revolution was no longer a revolution—the Australian government had forced every business, big and small, to evolve. And so, in 2001, the market for Complete Business Results had almost completely disappeared.

John faced his first major business failure and was forced to close the business, but was fortunate enough to get a new job working as the CEO for his accounting software supplier in Sydney.

After six months of working as an employee once again, John made a successful bid to take over their Australian operations as their sole distributor and become a self-employed entrepreneur again. Within a few years, with annual revenues in excess of $2.5 million (nearly 80% recurring), they became #2 in the world for a major accounting software brand.

About the Author

He learned a lot about developing recurring revenue, software development, negotiation, marketing, sales, and people management throughout these years.

In 2013, John sold the distribution company to focus on his new venture, "Evolve Systems", which provided digital marketing services for clients. Along the way, he became a hybrid book publisher and was involved in publishing over 2,000 books.

His next venture, evolvepreneur.app, will draw on all of his previous experience and then some!

Evolvepreneur.app's mission statement is to start a revolution that will help entrepreneurs establish their own complete business system that can compete with mainstream social media platforms.

His goal is to help move entrepreneurs away from being a cog in the machine, and instead create their own machine!

Our Startup Framework

How To Create Specific Strategies To Build Your List, Make Offers And Connect With Your Best Buyes

- Mindset
- Strategy
- Implementation
- Measure & Review
- Pivot & Repeat

My Entrepreneurial Journey

"When everything seems to be going against you, remember that the airplane takes off against the wind, not with it."

—**Henry Ford, founder of Ford Motor Company.**

My journey to becoming an entrepreneur and marketer started quite young. I was about ten years old when I started my first business. I worked in my mother's post office franchise and decided to sell eggs from our chickens. We had a lot of regular customers who came into the post office—easy target market!

Of course, at that age, I knew nothing about business or marketing. But that also meant I had no fear or previous failures to hold me back. I just asked everyone I saw if they wanted to buy some eggs. Business was booming, and I had several recurring customers, which meant sometimes demand outstripped supply! I learned a lesson in only selling what I had and not promising more than I could deliver. But one day, something bad happened—well, for a ten-year-old, it was awful!

My mother decided that I shouldn't keep all the profits and said I should pay for the chicken feed. For me, that was bad because, at $2 a dozen, it wasn't much money. So I made a decision and closed the egg business down. I felt if I couldn't make 100%, it wasn't worth it. It's funny how, today, business owners will keep stripping away their profits to the point they make very little but won't make any strategic changes that could turn around their business, or perhaps even avoid bankruptcy.

Looking back, when I was young, I didn't realize that I was destined to create my own business ventures. I would set up and create pretend businesses and even set up a shop. I put stock out, created pretend sales, and recorded it all down in my accounts. Part of the reason for all of this was that I was living near a remote railway station with a few houses around it in the middle of Queensland, Australia, with a population of around five to ten people at any given time. Because I did School of the Air, which is a remote way of attending school, I had a lot more time on my hands without a lot of other children around.

By the time I was fourteen, we had moved to a small town not far away. The population was around five-hundred people, and I went to a local high school. But I managed to get a part-time job packing vegetables at a local supermarket. I would rush to my job immediately after school to get as many hours in as I could to earn more money. My goal at the time was to buy an expensive watch, and the only way to do that was to earn money myself.

My boss was so impressed with my work ethic he wanted to pay me to go to years 11 and 12 at boarding school. His family was wealthy and owned a few businesses in the town, but I hated school, and the thought of living away from home and going to school didn't appeal to me. So I told him I didn't want to do it.

I left school as quickly as I could, at age fifteen, which was the end of year 10. I walked out of the school gates, never to return. I went to the local government employment agency and registered my name. Little did I know, no-one else from my class had thought to do that. Maybe they had jobs lined up. And so, when the local Westpac Bank decided they needed a new trainee, they dropped in to see who was registered. The bank was right next door to the employment agency!

They contacted me, and I sat a test and managed to convince them to hire me! I look at my son who at the time of writing is nearly 18, and is two years older than I was at the time and wonder what they were thinking! I must have looked so young!

I went on to work for the bank in several branches and roles over the next twelve years. Along the way, I trained as an ambulance and state emergency services officer. I even received an Australia Day award for services to the local community.

The training the bank provided was excellent; it showed me so much about systems, processes, customer service, and even marketing. Banks have a very defined way of doing business, and everything is documented and monitored. Because the bank paid for external education as well, I decided to do an Associate Diploma in Business (Accounting). It was a long course, over 24 modules spanning four years. But I liked it, and many of the lecturers were hands-on, which meant it was real-world learning.

Once I had passed, I was also able to become a qualified Public Accountant. I never became an accountant, but the skills I learned helped me go on to open my own part-time business.

It was in 1989 when I started getting very interested in the emerging computer revolution and founded this part-time computer and accounting software business. I realized the huge opportunity that was fast emerging, so I focused on building this business.

Finally, I was back on the path of being my own boss. I decided to help small-business owners keep track of their accounts. This was back in the early '90s when computers had first become accessible, and accounting software was being offered to the masses.

It didn't take me long before I had thirty customers while simultaneously holding down a full-time job at the bank. Then came a game changer…the mobile phone was invented! For a mere $3,000, you could have a Motorola flip phone. It wasn't much bigger than the current iPhone, but it had a bigger battery. If you talked for too long, it would nearly burn your ear off!

But this gave me freedom, even at $2 a minute for phone calls, which meant I could spend my lunch hour calling prospects and closing deals. It didn't take me long to realize this was a real opportunity. With computers becoming mainstream, a strong demand for software, and not a lot of people around to help implement and train them, I decided to quit my job at the bank and start a full-time business in 1991.

We grew fast, and by early 2000, we had a significant market share in the North Queensland city where I had been transferred to by the bank. I had made strategic partnerships with local computer retailers to provide their clients with software and training. But then one of the leading retailers went out of business, and because I hadn't had to do any marketing, it put me at high risk.

So I set myself on a path of learning; I spent the next three years and over $100,000 learning about marketing my business. By the time I finished, I had grown the business from just myself to over five staff and heading towards $1.5 million in turnover.

But something else took place in Australia in 1999; the government decided to bring out GST, which was a new tax system. It meant huge opportunities for us, as many businesses couldn't avoid computerization, but it also meant that most of the potential buyers were stripped out of the market in under a year. This caused a substantial post-GST slump, and business confidence plunged. My business dropped by 80% overnight; the day after the tax came in. It didn't show any signs of picking up anytime soon. It didn't take long for me to get caught with high overheads and low income.

So, for the first time since I had left the bank over nine years ago, I decided to get a job.

I got an offer from my accounting software supplier. The Managing Director was leaving and suggested I apply for his role. The recruitment process took six months, and I had to continue to operate my failing business in the meantime. It taught me how to look at a business very differently. Because my mindset was about the future, but we needed the money to pay the bills, we just persisted day-to-day.

Each morning, my sole remaining staff member and I would have a meeting and ask ourselves: "Should we close the business today?" We would look at each other and mutually decide to give it another day.

It was one of the most stressful times of my life, but eventually, I managed to get the job in Sydney in 2000 and relocated to start in January 2001 as Managing Director of the local Pastel accounting distribution. They later merged with Sage.

It only took six months before I was self-employed again. The business wasn't doing well when I took over, and despite being able to turn a small profit, Pastel didn't want to continue in Australia. However, I saw this as a class #1 opportunity.

Microsoft Windows had started to become more popular than DOS-based systems, and I knew this would be a new world for business.

So they agreed to let me have the existing business and resellers and continue as an independent distributor. What happened in the next twelve years is worthy of a book in itself. To cut a long story short, we became the 2nd-highest selling distributor for Sage Pastel globally out of 60 distributors and created a recurring income base of over $2.5M that represented nearly 80% of our normal revenue.

But nothing lasts forever, and a twist of fate meant we sold our interests in 2012 and decided to start our new Evolve Systems brand, designed to empower small business people to get better at marketing and sales. Along the way, we became a hybrid book publisher and were involved in publishing more than 2,000 books.

My Entrepreneurial Journey

The fortunate part of the new business was that we did have customers from the old business using some of our hosting and software services. This allowed us to have some cash flow coming through, but it became very apparent that the old customers weren't our new customers. While they gave us a foundation to help pay the bills, we had to focus on a better future vision.

And in fact, my first client was an electrician. He came around to quote me on some work for my house, and somehow, I ended up pitching him marketing services while he was on my roof! We came up with a domain name and business strategy while he was doing my wiring.

Then he asks me the closing question...

"How much?"

At this stage, I didn't even have a price list, so I said:

"How about $500 a month?"

Of course, he jumped at it, and I learned a very important lesson about pricing this type of service.

I then set out to tackle his business. He had nothing - not even a website. So we built websites, free reports, a mobile app, created google and Facebook ads, as well as social media accounts on all of the important mainstream platforms. Then came branding, social media posts, and CRM (client relationship management software).

I realized at the time that I didn't know much about marketing online. So I went to trusty Google to look for information and came across a course by Ed Rush and Mike Koenigs, which provided me with all the resources I needed. I was able to adapt their ideas and incorporate my previous life as a computer consultant in the creation of *EvolveYourBusiness.co*

The next person I pitched for the same service per month was $2,500, then $5,000, and finally $10,000. We had over 6 clients at this stage plus various other one-off marketing services. The agreement was that they had to stick with us for 12 months because of the amount of time we needed to get it all done.

This process taught me a valuable lesson about perceived value and what clients really want.

This business continued to grow to around $500k within the first six months with clients from a plumbing, lawn mowing, financial services and large security business. The challenge was that we wanted to do so much for our clients, but we found that it was a massive amount of work. As a long-term business model, in my mind, it wasn't viable.

But the knowledge I learned from the process of doing other people's marketing was invaluable. For any new business I create, my focus is always on recurring revenue. Most businesses rely solely on getting a new customer every time to keep the doors open. To me, this is crazy if you do the math. Acquiring a new customer is expensive.

It was only ever intended as a marketing experiment, and after 12 months, we slowly closed off the monthly clients, and to this day, we still service many of these clients, but their foundation was set.

During this process, I realized that one of the most powerful ways to market your business is to write a book.

By chance, one of my suppliers of lead capture pages and autoresponder software offered a course about publishing books at the same time. This sparked an idea for a whole new business.

This choice leads us to become a book publisher and empower authors to get their message out to the marketplace. I then wrote two books: *What Most Business Owners Don't Know And Will Never Know About Internet Marketing* and *Everything You Know About Marketing Is Wrong!* and launched them to become #1 International Best Sellers on Amazon. We created a new business called EvolveGlobalPublishing.com, and to date, we have helped over 150 authors create and launch their books.

I am always a firm believer that, if I am going to offer services to people, I need to make sure they have been tested on myself first. I don't believe you have a right to help people to market their businesses unless you have first tried your ideas on yourself.

So we started to merge what we learned from marketing offline businesses and adopted it for our new authors and myself. What I realized was that we needed a way to generate leads for the books and ultimately fill sales funnels for their backend services and products.

I looked to social media and decided to start with LinkedIn. I spent a few months mastering the platform and implementing all sorts of automated software.

The process was pretty simple: view profiles, connect with people, and send a welcome message offering my book for free. I was starting to fill up my funnel with prospects, but this meant I needed some kind of autoresponder to follow up.

This started another journey with using a new product on the market called Clickfunnels, and a CRM called Agile CRM.

Using the concept of being my own experiment, I built over 100 funnels and email marketing campaigns to complement the process. I tested all sorts of offers and studied a lot of online marketers. I spent tens of thousands of dollars on courses and coaching. I have to admit to being a sufferer of PSOS, or the Pretty Shiny Objects Syndrome, and went on many tangents, pursuing the latest great idea. This is where most entrepreneurs get lost in the weeds. They tend to jump at these shiny objects without any thought toward overall strategy or implementation.

I recall a friend of mine who sold business planning software. The reality was that most of the people who bought it put the software box on their bookshelf and never even installed it!

Why?

Because, in their mind, just by having bought it, they had already solved the problem. I suggest that the same is happening when you buy that next online information product.

I learned all about strategy, landing pages, membership sites, email marketing, webinars, social media, and so much more.

We then offered our services globally and realized the power of LinkedIn opened up conversations with prospects all over the world. Ultimately, we designed a system called the "90 Day Marketing Challenge", which was compression of everything I discovered over the course of my self-experimental journey.

After helping over 150 entrepreneurs, it became apparent that to make any substantial difference, I needed a better way of offering our knowledge to a lot more people. In pursuit of this, I wrote the *5 Stages To Entrepreneurial Success and Book Publishing Secrets For Entrepreneurs*, which would serve as the foundation for my next venture.

Most recently, I was involved as one of the 15 authors of *Authority: Strategic Concepts from 15 International Thought Leaders to Create Influence, Credibility and a Competitive Edge for You and Your Business*. To find out more about this book, visit authoritythebook.com.

What I also learned was that, like many entrepreneurs, it's really easy to start a business, but focusing on making it highly successful requires time and energy.

I woke up one morning on a long weekend, and it all came to me. I sat on my patio for over 4 hours and wrote over ten pages of notes. To me, it was amazing, because it was as if everything had fallen into place.

I created Evolvepreneur.club, which is designed to bring many of my needs together. Primarily, to help more entrepreneurs to become successful by providing a system and process they can follow, but at the same time leverage our system so that it's scalable to hundreds of thousands of people.

My next need was having a business that I could experiment on and use everything I learned so far in 25+ years in business. Evolvepreneur.club gives me the freedom to continue my journey without starting a new business when I get bored.

The major challenge that most online business owners face is providing a world-class website experience, as it can be complicated and expensive. It often means cobbling several solutions together using plugins and third-party tools to get a functioning website capable of engaging and convincing visitors to buy from you.

As the number of businesses relying on the internet for day-to-day operations has grown, a new type of software system has arisen. It's called SaaS - Software as a Service.

I remember when I first started selling accounting software - you often had to buy multiple unconnected products to manage your cashbook, invoicing, payroll, and asset management. Over time, these functions merged into powerful, interconnected single-system solutions at a fraction of the cost of all the individual components.

Individually, these systems often are costly and labour-intensive to maintain. When I started working for clients in digital marketing, if I ran into a problem, I knew there was "an app for that". Whilst this is great, it also opens your business up to problems if one app fails or someone misses an update or forgets to sync all of these unconnected applications.

I believe the next-level SaaS "social platform" or "all-in-one business system" will be a significant opportunity in the marketplace for entrepreneurs.

If you want to create a real growth-based sustainable business, my advice is to focus on building your own complete system; become independent from

"Big Tech" so you can't be banned or throttled. Use them to send traffic to your own assets like a website, recurring membership, online e-commerce shop, or e-learning platform, and build your own audience.

As a marketing consultant, after thousands of hours of consulting and deploying marketing systems, the following is a blueprint for what I believe a typical online entrepreneur needs to be successful in today's highly-competitive marketplace:

Your major focus should be on the overall customer experience. You will also want to try to be as frictionless as possible throughout. At the same time, employ as much automation as possible.

You should start with a mobile-ready website that tightly integrates your content-based assets, such as your podcast channel, on-demand videos, courses, memberships, and blogs.

Seamlessly build up your subscriber database and automatically email subscribers when new content is available. Your marketing module should trigger emails or actions based on your prospect's behaviour, as well as help them progress through your courses and products.

You will need to design some pages to promote free checklists, blueprints, and/or ebooks to build your subscriber database. You will want your visitors to be able to buy your products & services and handle the delivery of your digital download or physical product on the same site. At the same time, you may wish to upsell products at checkout.

By segmenting your prospects, you can build powerful followup emails.

You should have multiple payment gateways. This reduces the risk of one portal withholding funds if you grow too fast. You could also sell products in different currencies to lower buyer resistance.

You may want the ability to create a recurring membership system where you can charge users at regular intervals and allow them to easily update their records with you.

You may want different front-end websites, but they should all lead back to your eCommerce and backend member area so you can manage them easily. This allows you to promote different angles of your business without splitting up your audience or resources.

To grow your business, you should create an affiliate program and encourage referrers or affiliates to share your products and services for rewards.

At the end of the process, the prospect or customer should finish their initial journey in your back-end membership area, which includes all of their invoices, downloads, and bonus content. You don't want your customers fumbling around with separate websites looking for all of this information!

It's vital to have a ticketing system or similar service system to support your customers.

The next step is to create a highly-engaged community for your clients and prospects that provides the extra value behind a secure login and keeps them coming back for your content. To further engage users, you need to gamify your community through status badges and rewards systems.

Think about creating courses where your members can learn online at their own pace. Your course system should allow them to progress step-by-step as they do each lesson, not necessarily on a weekly release schedule where they could quickly get behind and give up. You should also encourage students to engage with other students.

What if they didn't need to download a worksheet PDF they never actually complete? You need a system to allow them to leave their responses as they work through the lessons. This will give you the ability to see all their answers, which means you also know where they are in the course. This means no one is left behind! A useful feature is to be able to assign a task to your students as they progress through the course. You could also create a coaching program based on their task list.

You also need a powerful analytics reporting a system that tells you exactly where your traffic is coming from and what they're clicking on to help make decisions for your marketing campaigns.

You will also want a single dashboard to view statistics, create content, and manage your business.

Ideally, you should build a procedure system (Knowledge Base) so your staff and outsourcers can run your processes the same way every time. Make it easy to create step-by-step instructions rather than having to continually re-train staff.

What if you wanted to create a mastermind group? It would be best if you could group people together and allow users to be able to access Q&A calls, group tasks, and results in a logical and centralized way.

It would also help to have a project management system to help you and your team manage your projects as well as client ones. Most importantly, your platform needs to have fast loading times, or you risk driving customers away!

How long do you think it would take to implement all of this?

Maybe a year or longer!

I've spent thousands of dollars and many fruitless hours in search of the best all-in-one platform that had most of the features I wanted. But as far as I could tell, that system doesn't exist. In frustration, I set out on a journey to develop my own unique platform, completely based around the needs of entrepreneurs, coaches, consultants, authors, podcasters, publishers, and mastermind groups.

I called it evolvepreneur.app. My mission is to start a revolution to help entrepreneurs establish their own complete business system that can compete with mainstream social media platforms.

Don't become a cog in the machine; create your own machine.

I challenge you to focus on building your own complete business community platform.

Take control of your destiny and sleep better a night!

We've come full circle, and you might notice a trend here. Success leaves clues, right? The first thing I did was to write a book, which is the one you are reading right now. This is the start of your journey with me; I hope this book will give you ideas and strategies to move to the next stage and ultimately become a Time Master!

I encourage you to take a look at our Evolvepreneur.club website to add even more value to this book.

Introduction

So, you have decided to create a new business, or maybe add an extra product or service. Perhaps you are looking for a seachange.

This is the starting point for any new entrepreneur. It's where the magic happens. In order to get from an idea to a product/service/business, you need to make sure your concept has a solid foundation. This is always an exciting part of your journey, but you also need to be realistic about what is possible and what financial or physical barriers you will have to overcome to get your idea to the next stage.

Discover how to fast track your idea to startup without risking large amounts of capital investment. Learn how to create your own marketing strategies to quickly test your market and grow your idea with our 5-step system.

The startup stage is your foundation. If your foundation is shaky, then the whole concept will be unstable as well. Most people spend very little time in this area and never commit to spending a few hours to really figure out their big picture strategy. Don't be one of them!

Our Startup Framework

Entrepreneurs struggle the most with implementation. They can often become frozen in time and start to over-complicate their idea.

In most cases, it's better to make a start and try than spend large chunks of time on a project that you aren't even sure will work.

This allows you to test the idea, try some different approaches and then scale it.

1 Mindset — It's important to imagine the outcome you want from a new project; visualise the best outcome for you and see yourself achieving it. Talk about it in the past tense as if it has already happened. Your mind doesn't know the difference! I know this sounds woo-woo, but getting your brain right first is important.

2 Strategy — This is a very important step that many entrepreneurs seem to want to skip. They get a great idea and rush a little too fast to the implementation stage. The rose-coloured glasses effect can be dangerous here. Looking at the big picture first and making sure that your idea is going to fit into your overall goals and considering the downside of it failing is time well spent before the actual implementation.

3 Implementation — This stage requires a good plan to ensure that you implement your project quickly and effectively. Entrepreneurs can get stuck here if they make this step overly complex or hit technical issues they can't solve. Sometimes, an entrepreneur takes on too much at once and projects are stalled and left unfinished. This is the biggest waste of their time and energy. A great way to implement a strategy is to think about it in terms of stages or versions. That way, you can focus on continual improvement rather than having everything done and perfect. You need a solid testing process, as well. There have been plenty of times where we have seen a marketing campaign rollout where the organizers never actually checked that the website was working or whether the next step worked. You can only imagine how many prospects this small failure can cost.

4 Measure & Review — The next vital step is to review the project and make sure it's hitting your original goals. Set realistic review dates and goals. Being able to measure results properly is vital; what gets measured gets improved.

5 Pivot & Repeat — In a lot of situations, it's very small changes that make a massive difference. You might think a marketing campaign has failed, but perhaps some simple changes in the headline or making sure that the site displays properly on mobile would make the difference in conversion. Always consider making small changes first before thinking that you need to start all over again. At the same time, don't be afraid to consider a pivot. There are many cases where the first idea never worked, but the feedback and review process found a different angle that ended up massively successful. Paypal started off as a security tool for palm pilots, and when faced with no response, they eventually pivoted to a payment system for eBay.

| 1 | **Mindset** |  |

| 2 | Strategy | |

| 3 | Implementation | |

| 4 | Measure & Review | |

| 5 | Pivot & Repeat | |

What is the Founder Stage?

"If you want to live an exceptional and extraordinary life, you have to give up many of the things that are part of a normal one."

—Srinivas Rao

So, you have decided to create a new business, or maybe you want to add an extra product or service to an existing business. Perhaps you are looking for a seachange.

The Founder stage is your foundation. If your foundation is shaky, then the whole concept will be unstable as well. Most people spend very little time in this area and never commit to spending a few hours to really figure out their big picture strategy. Don't be one of them!

In a recent 2-hour call with an author, where we discussed his personal branding and business strategy, he ended the call with this comment:

"I really should have done this before I spent $100k writing and publishing my book!"

Every day, we speak to entrepreneurs who are lost and can't understand why their business isn't working. They don't understand why customers come and go with no rhyme or reason, and why they can never maintain momentum. Almost every time, we find out that they've skipped over this step. A great idea hit them - an entrepreneurial seizure if you like - and they launched the business based on that idea, but didn't spend enough time laying the foundation for that business's success in the future.

A great book that every entrepreneur should read at least 10 times is *The E-Myth Revisited: Why Most Small Businesses Don't Work and What To Do About It*.

Of course, this book was written over 25 years ago, long before Google or the vast array of cloud-based solutions took hold of the digital space, but I believe the fundamentals still apply. Hiring staff and contractors is always a prominent area that entrepreneurs tend to fail spectacularly in.

Do you know what's strange?

Most people have no idea what they want, and what they say want is rarely what they think they want. Isn't that funny?

Most people, if they were honest with themselves, and they actually sat down and took the time to look at what they desired, would find that what they say and what they want is actually just a fraction or a facet of what they actually want. In some cases, it is the polar opposite of what they want.

Here are the Top 10 goals for a great business (courtesy of the Fortune Institute)

- Tightly-Run Financials
- Bigger Mission Than Money
- Systems-Oriented
- Training Culture
- Testing Emphasis
- Clear Point-of-Difference
- Clear Marketing Funnels
- Back-End Product
- Clear Understanding of Customers
- High-Productivity Environment

So, let's get to work now and start on your solid foundation with a few worksheets.

Grab a pen and paper now and let's get started...

So what are the best ways to make a fortune from scratch?

Here are some excerpts from Dan Kennedy's Book *How to Make Millions With Your Ideas*:

"Wealth is very often linked to exclusive ownership or control of a particular product or service, rather than being a part of someone else's business model.

One of the insider secrets to making millions is doing everything possible to minimise circumstances beyond your control.

Ordinary businesses can surprise you.

Consider businesses like dry cleaners, gift shops, and restaurants, who seem to have created a job for themselves and make nominal income. Somewhere in every one of these business categories is someone who has turned an ordinary business into an extraordinary profit-making machine.

The exciting truth is that you can take just about any ordinary business and manage the money very intelligently and that business will make you rich. The service category is a large business category.

Why?

Because at all levels of society, people are unbelievably pressed for time, so they need someone to do it for them. Incorporating a personal service element in any business or product will enable you to capitalize on this trend.

Go forth and multiply.

One of the greatest benefits of turning an ordinary business into an extraordinary profit-making machine and owning or controlling the products is the ability to get rich through duplication and multiplication.

Once there was one *McDonald's*, one subway shop, one of everything. Even the simplest of ideas for your products and services, properly-packaged, can make you wealthy through duplication and multiplication.

The concept of Direct Marketing is now one of the fastest-growing categories of business. It bypasses all the traditional complexity and costs of manufacturers' sales forces, wholesalers and other middlemen, retail stores or brand identity.

The most traded, most consumed, most sought after and the most valued commodity is not precious stones, oil or real estate. It is specialized information. The list of types of information being made into profits is almost endless. Fame and fortune do go together."

Making yourself famous as an expert is a low-cost way to save substantial money on marketing. For example, writing a book can position yourself quickly to a niche market.

One of Evolve System's companies is *EvolveGlobalPublishing.com*, where we can help someone create a #1 Best Selling Book in as little as 90 days without writing a single word!

Here are some key ideas to help determine your path to wealth…

Publicity is so powerful it can even build businesses with no proactive advertising.

Attain the market, then get the product (the reverse of most people's approach).

Pick products (and businesses) using proven criteria with your general interests.

Negotiate for limited, defined, exclusive rights in a win-win way for both parties.

If you don't ask, you don't get!

Charge premium prices and deliver premium value.

Lead your marketing with irresistible offers.

Create extra profit centers.

Diversify your marketing efforts.

Continually listen to your customers, then react and respond.

Deliberately build on customer loyalty.

Think big!

Design services that solve other people's most vexing problems.

Design services that save people time.

Specialise in your market.

Follow your talents. Systemise and grow.

Duplicate your knowledge, methods, and attitudes into others.

Turn your business or money-making system into a business opportunity in a box.

Go to the end user and build relationships with your customers.

Use your marketing as a way of collecting data about your customers.

Test, Test, Test.

Tap into other people's databases and established customer relationships.

The most in-demand, most consumed commodity of our time is information.

Packaging and selling information with an emphasis on publishing on demand gives you enormous financial leverage.

If you know how to, you have the basis for a profitable information marketing business.

Find a way to inject an element of outrageousness into your publicity.

> *"The critical ingredient is getting off your butt and doing something. It's as simple as that. A lot of people have ideas, but there are few who decide to do something about them now. Not tomorrow. Not next week. But today. The true entrepreneur is a doer, not a dreamer."*
>
> **–Nolan Bushnell, entrepreneur.**

It's a common question: what makes a successful entrepreneur?

Of course, this question sparks a whole conversation about the definition of success itself.

It's my belief that success isn't just about making money. Most people start a business for the freedom they expect it to give them. The cold hard reality is that most entrepreneurs end up working longer hours for far less than a typical wage.

Why would any sane person work much longer hours for less money, with way less freedom than they probably had in a day job?

The reason is they have a much bigger vision for their future than the average person. So, why is it that, if entrepreneurs work harder than an average worker, not every entrepreneur becomes massively successful?

What is the secret that ensures the budding entrepreneur becomes successful?

It's probably a cliche, but there is a formula to it. The challenge is that there are plenty of mad scientists out there trying to sell you their own secret formula. Often, it only works fully for them and a few followers.

Why?

Survivor bias. Most of these mad scientists don't set out to deceive every entrepreneur looking for a roadmap to success; many of them are selling you the method that they think got them where they are today, even if the method has a low success rate. Or maybe their method had very little impact on what actually made them successful, and they don't realise it.

There are no real shortcuts to success, though, of course, there are exceptions to the rule. It's called luck or being at the right place at the right time. But often, even the overnight success stories actually have a hard-luck backstory and years of failure and frustration.

This book is about the process, strategy and implementation of your ideas. The 5 stages is our way of presenting to you a viable success path and will help you understand the mindset you need to develop to achieve your definition of success.

You may be tempted to diagnose yourself at one stage and skip the stages prior. The reality is that, often, the problems and challenges that come back to haunt you are due to a lack of concentration on the fundamentals.

Try to work through your business from stage 1 to stage 5 first. If you feel you have achieved the necessary steps for that stage, feel free to skip ahead.

Here are the 5 stages to success in the new entrepreneurial world in our view…

Founder - this is the starting point for any new entrepreneur. It's where the magic happens. In order to get from an idea to a product/service/business, you need to make sure your concept has a solid foundation. This is always the most exciting part of your journey, but you also need to be realistic about what is possible and what financial or physical barriers you will have to push through to get your idea to the next stage.

Explorer - this stage is where an entrepreneur starts their search for the resources they need to get their idea to market. You need to consider things like what software you will be using for websites, eCommerce, autoresponders, and contact management. You need to consider how your idea will look in terms of branding, pricing and delivery. What staff and other contractors will you need to sell your products or service? Who can you attract to help you in terms of referral, affiliates or business partners?

Organiser - this is the vital stage that many entrepreneurs get stuck on. The successful implementation of their ideas is very important and can lead to lost opportunities, or even worse, project failure. If their choices are not solid in the explorer stage, they often end up struggling with the technology side of their business. They can also invest too much in the wrong solutions, leaving only a small amount of money to actually promote their business. They need to find the right people to help them or ensure they understand the solutions they need to implement. Automation is the key at this stage. Anything you can do to remove manual handling or staff involvement, the better you will be long term.

Investor - this stage is where the entrepreneur is focused on growing their business and investing time and money to see the idea launched into the marketplace. Often, entrepreneurs will give up too early or start to second guess themselves at this stage. In addition, if their marketing and sales systems are not in place for automation, then processes start to break and too much time is spent on putting out fires. This is the time to start measuring everything you can in your business and plan for your future or exit.

Time-Master - for any entrepreneur, having the time to do what they want, when they want and with whom they want is their ultimate goal. At this stage, you are focused on only spending time on what you are good at or what you want to do, and the systems and processes handle the backend of your business. Now is the time to leverage your business at the next level, sell it, or bring in partners or investors.

Each stage has its own chapter and processes. This book is designed not only to educate you but to give you the tools to come back and apply a chapter when you need it the most.

This book is designed to give you a foundation for your business. If you believe you want even more, feel free to get in touch with me. We're passionate about helping business people, and there is nothing better than seeing the smiling face of a business owner in charge of his own destiny who has mastered the art of marketing.

We have really only touched the surface with this book, and it is my hope that it encourages you to dig further.

In this book, we will reveal the strategies you can immediately deploy that will enable you to out-think, out-market and out-sell your competition.

So, let's dive in and get started on your journey...

Your Primary Mission

Your "primary mission" is not about your business; it's about you. It's a short statement that pushes you to get out of bed in the morning. It's not about material assets; it's the essence of your purpose.

The "primary mission" is very personal. The best way to know you have figured out your primary mission is that the statement makes you feel full of energy and commitment.

It gives you a sense of "that's me!" Your primary mission gives you the ability to live your life on purpose, rather than by accident.

It's unique. It's truly about what you want for yourself. It's all about you; put aside thoughts of putting other people first, your primary purpose already exists within you.

The discovery process:
- List what you don't want in your life
- List what you DO want in your life
- Set priorities and bust barriers
- Write your eulogy
- Write your primary mission

Write a short phrase or sentence but no more than a couple of sentences expressing the core of what you want your life to be all about.

When you write it, you should feel the energy, enthusiasm, commitment, and a sense of, "yes, that's me".

If not, you haven't gotten it yet. Keep trying.

The Importance of Goal-Setting

"All successful people have a goal. No one can get anywhere unless they know where they want to go and what they want to be or do."

—Norman Vincent Peale.

Achieving targets and goals is a major challenge in the life of every entrepreneur. No matter how well you do, there will always be a desire for more.

Setting goals are not only a way to accomplish your entrepreneurial success, but it is also an essential human need. If you want to fill your life with purpose and accomplishment, you need to start with worthwhile goals that are most important to you. Just getting through the day is not enough. The ability to set goals correctly is a skill that can be learned and implemented.

The good news is that goal-setting does work, and it works because you have a brain that operates as a mechanical goal-seeking device.

Possessing and achieving goals is what separates us from all other forms of life. Once you have set a goal and started trying to achieve it, you need to make sure you stay on target. Constantly check your progress and when necessary, change or correct your actions to ensure you stay on target.

You build your life and your success by your thoughts, and the first step to building yourself is a winning self-concept. Who you believe you are and who you are is your potential.

What you believe will become reality (if you have faith in your mind's goal-seeking mechanism)

What you believe grows from an idea, a vision or dream into reality in your life. If you dwell on your eventual success, you will achieve it. Focus on problems in a negative way, and they will grow and overwhelm you. The images you see will become real. The more often you concentrate on them, the sooner you will attain them.

When setting your goals, focus on the result or outcome rather than the actual process.

Focusing on outcomes is a critical element if you want to succeed. Try to avoid making your goal smaller. You may have to compromise, which is a fact of life. The trick is to pay the right price for the right thing.

You also need to write down your goals otherwise you can easily change them in your mind!

Some ideas:
- What are my lifetime goals?
- What would I like my situation to be in 5 years from now?
- What would I like my situation to be in 3 years from now?
- What is the most important current ambition?

Goals should be written in result terms rather than activity terms. Eg.

Activity Terms

I want to learn more about our new Product Y.

Result Terms

I want to sell 10 of our new product Y within 30 days.

The message here is clear. You may learn and know more about Product Y than anyone else.

The whole purpose of writing goals in result terms is to achieve a positive result. A goal must then be tested for validity. Try to write down in result terms, focused on achieving a positive and worthwhile result that is specific. Output forces you to focus and to act.

A few ideas to help achieve your goals…

Balance your picture – ask yourself whether your goals fit your total lifestyle picture.

Align your goals – this means working in an orderly and consistent way. Smaller goals should work towards achieving bigger long-term goals.

Co-operate with others – if others are involved, and you need cooperation, ask for it. Most people are glad to help. Be prepared to return the favor for their goals in the future.

Visualise what you want, not what you want to avoid – This law of life is critical to your success. At all times, focus on what you want until it becomes the dominant thought. If you visualize what you don't want, it becomes the dominant thought and this is what you will surely get! This is why so many of life's negative people get what they least want. They focus on what they fear, rather than on what they desire.

Have a clear image of what you want – traditional goal-achieving methods don't take into account of the power of your mind and the role that visualization plays. If you want to succeed, you must acquire the skill of visualization and back it up with belief in and understanding of the part it plays. If you can't see it, you can't do it.

Accept Responsibility – It's up to you. If you don't do it, it won't get done. It's your goal; it's your responsibility. Once you accept absolute responsibility for your actions and your goals, you will look at life differently. Actions will take on a whole new meaning; options will look real, possibilities unfold that you hadn't seen before. This is the power of choice to determine what you want. However, before you can exercise this right or power, it is necessary to be in charge of yourself. Set time for accomplishment – "I will have it done by ….[date]." Nothing generates action more than effectively setting a date by which a goal is to be accomplished.

Measure your achievement – It's important to define clearly how you will know when you have accomplished your goal. You need to measure what has been done. It is vital it's recorded in a way that others can also understand. Since you often need others to help you achieve your goals.

Check your progress – Set dates of review. Be constantly checking how you are going, where you are going, and whether you are on time; on the plan. If not, why not? How do you plan to get back on target again? If you simply take things as they come, it is almost guaranteed that you will achieve less than you could.

Write down the "how-to" of your plan – put your goals in writing. That's the vital key. Then prepare a detailed activity plan to achieve your goals. You need a separate activity plan for each goal you set. The real issue isn't what you want; the real issue is how to get what you want. Until you write out a list of activities to carry out to achieve your goal, you are largely only dealing with the "want to", without strong desire nothing will be achieved.

Many people believe they can keep their goals in their head. Let's say you have 6 goals, which have 10-20 activities for each goal to achieve them. On average, that's 15 activities for each goal, which need to be carried out in sequence. This means a total of 90 activities; some may even be mini-goals in themselves! Do you believe you can handle 90 activities in your head? If you don't write down your goals and activities, you will have to do them as they occur to you, taking a chance you will get it right.

Write them in the future tense.

Now that we have spoken about Goal-Setting, apart from setting personal goals, you also need to set goals for your business.

One of the biggest problems in any business is the owner!

Yes, you… Why?

Because you don't necessarily have anyone keeping you honest with your business goals. You can always make a trade-off in your mind and make excuses. Would you accept some of these excuses from a staff member?

Probably not. In fact, you might even consider firing them!

If you want your business to grow, you need to decide how it will look when it's finished. That was part of the reason that in Level One, you wrote down your "Strategic Objective". Start with the end in mind and figure out where you want to be in 3, 5, and 10 years.

Remember, if you are not following your plan, you are probably following someone else's. And what do they have planned for you? Usually not much!

What and When!

Set some time frames for when your business will grow in terms of turnover, clients, billing time etc. Once you reach these targets then look at putting some into your business that can take over some of your daily functions. A great book to read BEFORE employing anyone is the E-Myth by Gerber. Essentially, you need to prepare your business for new employees, not wait until you find someone good and hope it all works out (which, by the way, is 90% of what most business people do).

The best way to start is to fill out an organizational chart with each key "job position" and then complete a job description for each position. Sign it. Once you know which each position is set about documenting it, so when you are prepared to hire someone for that position then you can simply hand it over. Don't ever hire someone on their skills and then create a position for them.

It's a recipe for disaster. You will end up doing whatever they don't want to do.

After all, who is the boss?

The side benefit of documentation is that your business becomes much more saleable, in fact, clients feel more comfortable when they know how you run your business. It can be used as a selling tool. I often showed a prospect our client training system checklist and manual or even our job descriptions.

In some cases, they don't even have it in their business, and instantly it gives them confidence that you know what you are doing.

Goal-Writing Workshop

Choose a Goal that you wish to achieve in the next 12 months:

Write down the "how to" aspects of this goal (the small things you need to achieve the BIGGER goal:

1._____WHEN:

2._____WHEN:

3._____WHEN:

4._____WHEN:

What Are Your Personal Objectives?

It's very important to set your own personal targets that should eventually align with your business needs. Otherwise, you run the risk of the business's needs overtaking your personal lifestyle.

Make your goals a bit harder long-term; don't underplay the future by making them too conservative.

Personal Objectives

Component	3-6 months	Next Year	In 5 years	10 years +
Annual Income				
Professional Growth				
Education & Personal Development				
Family and Relationships				
Hobbies, Pastimes				
Travel, Leisure				
Retirement				
Major Purchases				

Action Steps and Summary

Congratulations, you made it!

Most people brush over this critical stage because it's hard work. Without a clear idea of your mission, goals, and personal objectives, you will likely wander the path but never really know if you're going in the right direction!

Commit to yourself that you will come back and review your completed worksheets and statements at least once a year.

Action Steps:

Find time to fill out the worksheets in this chapter; don't just do them in your head!

Build out your next action steps on paper and then set them up in your diary.

Chapter Summary:

Discover your primary mission and live it every day!

Make plans for your future – "if you are not following your plan, you are following someone else's!"

Do this process every year or so to make sure you are still on-track.

Now that we've covered the mindset you should have when building and maintaining your business, let's move onto strategy.

This is when the fun starts!

1 Mindset

2 Strategy

3 Implementation

4 Measure & Review

5 Pivot & Repeat

Developing a Strategic Objective

What is your strategic objective?

Your strategic objective is a precise written statement of what your business will look like when it's complete. It's a detailed picture of the future – your vision of how your business will look, act, and perform.

Again, this subject is too big for one chapter. Instead, we will go over the concepts and leave it up to you to create this statement after this module.

Below is an example of a Strategic Objective:

"XYZ Computer Services is a service-oriented company providing high-quality business software and computer hardware solutions to Australia's small business owners on-time and within budget, every time. Our clients see us a problem solvers and the key to their business success through access to critical business information and savings in efficiency.

Our clients have a strong connection with us as they appreciate our attention to detail and personalized service. They feel we are more than a software or computer supplier, they treat us like a business partner and often cite our company as fundamental in the success of their business. We will inspire our clients to dramatically increase their efficiency and profitability for their business.

XYZ Computer Services' target market is represented by small to medium sized businesses with 2 to 50 employees. Typically, our clients are the owners who are also responsible for the day-to-day running of the business. Many industries are serviced, including commerce, service, retail, and manufacturing, and often our clients are at the start of their growth stage. The majority of system sales are financed through the company's Technology Rental Plan which provides for regular two-yearly rollovers which allow our clients to keep up with technology without the high cost of replacement.

XYZ Computer Services will be a premier provider of business systems and software Australia-Wide within the next five years.

By June XXXX, with annual sales in excess of $5M and a net profit rate of 20%, the company will be floated on the Australian Stock Exchange to fund further expansion into global markets and establishment of in-house Rental Finance facility. XYZ Computer Services will have a full-time staff (in Sydney) of 25 with a network of 50 commission-based consultants in key geographical areas Australia-wide.

For our company to achieve success, our primary influencers' needs must be satisfied. The four primary influencers are our customers, our employees, our suppliers and our lenders. Each of these groups will prefer to choose us over all other companies. Our company's systems will be far superior to our competition. Because of our company's ability to control our systems, we will be able to encourage customers to choose us over other competitors, generate the highest profit margins in the computer industry, pay the highest salaries in the industry, pay all of our suppliers on time, every time, and pay all of our lenders on time and within credit terms.

XYZ Computer Services will have a reputation for employing quality staff and creating a work environment envied by its competitors. Staff incentive and recreation policies will be well above industry standards and the subject of favourable comparison against our competitors.

Goods and services are delivered to our clients using an innovative and comprehensive module-based training system. Our training system is delivered through a series of workbooks, audios, telephone conference calls, and on-site visits from our consultants.

Every client will receive professional service from every department within the company. The company will be known for its neat and highly-organized staff. Every aspect of the company's operation is standardized and tightly controlled.

High-quality telephone and remote support are provided by our centralized HelpDesk Centre. Each support call is tracked and monitored and problems resolved within 2 hours.

All of our people wear distinctive corporate wardrobe. XYZ Computer Services is known in the marketplace for its innovative use of technology to assist small business to achieve success in areas of computerization and profitability.

XYZ Computer Services continually seeks the input of staff and customers to improve its efficiency and creates an atmosphere of a success-driven company."

Your Strategic Objective should have the following elements:
- Basic Characteristics
- Line of business and products offered
- Company Size and Growth Objectives
- Geographic Scope (business location, markets)
- Target Markets and Market PositioningTiming (years to completion)
- The Basis of Competition (what will be your competitive advantage?)
- Distinguishing/Unique Characteristics
- Distinctive elements of your product or service
- Distinctive Marketing Methods
- Distinctive Behaviour/Dress/Qualifications of Employees
- Distinctive OperationsOther Unique or Distinctive Characteristics

Your Strategic Objective is like a mini-business plan. Something that will stand the test of time and is easy to read by all interested parties. The old rule is that if it isn't written down it's meaningless and easy to change!

Who is our target market?

One of the single biggest mistakes most entrepreneurs make is trying to sell something to everyone. For example, when we sold accounting software, it was to a niche market.

Businesses are so diverse that you cannot expect someone to be an expert on every type of business. In my 10 years as an IT consultant, we would have sold systems to 500+ different businesses.

However, they can all be rolled into several "groups":
- Repair/Service Industry
- Retail Businesses
- Business to Business
- Manufacturing Enterprises including importers and exporters

A subset of the remainder was:
- Larger Corporate Businesses with local branches
- National Franchise Businesses with reporting requirements
- Clubs (e.g. RSL) with heavy general ledger requirements. General Businesses with more complex operations or requirements

The business "specialized" in this type of customer:
- Owner/s and working in the business day to day
- Growing business with 2-15 staff
- Desire to improve their business
- Generally, the business was around 2-5 years old and had been started by the current owner/s
- Retail and Service Industry amounted to 80% of our client base

It is vital to work out who your ideal customer is and look actively for them. This is represented in your advertising and marketing efforts. A poorly-defined target market is the single biggest reason why your marketing will not work. Likely you will get a lot of calls or emails representing a lot of time with little to no result. You need to know how your prospective customer thinks and feels, what their problems are, how they feel about you and your competitors. These are known as psychographic characteristics. Additionally, you need to know their demographic characteristics, such as age, sex, occupation, habits, and lifestyles.

Some questions to ask about your ideal prospect.
- Corporate – "Who are they?"
- Size
- Expanding
- Products
- Location
- Turnover
- Market
- Profit
- Competition
- Decision-Makers
- Staff Numbers

Psychographic – "How they think"

About your prospect or decision-maker:
- What are their concerns and problems?
- What do they want from life?
- What makes them feel good?
- What's their biggest problem that you can solve?
- What are their priorities for their money?
- What do they want for themselves?

About your products/service:
- Do they really want or do they really need it?
- What are their concerns about it?
- What problems does it answer?
- Where does it rate in their thinking?
- What will it really do for them?

Answer this for both you and your competition:
- What do they like?
- What do they dislike about?
- Why would they choose?
- How do they perceive?
- Why would they buy?
- What is unique and special about them?

Demographic – "How they measure up":
- Age Range?
- Owners/manages/works in the business?
- Sex?
- Marital?
- Education level?
- Job/Title?Industry?
- Income?
- Reads what newspapers?
- Reads what magazines?
- Belongs to Clubs/Associations/Communities?

Creating a Business Plan

Gone are the days of massive business plans that detail every aspect of an enterprise. The world simply moves so fast that a 5-year plan is rendered obsolete a few weeks after it's written.

Even 6-month, plans can be thrown out just as quickly as they were written.

So, how does the average entrepreneur cope in an uncertain world with no actual plans?

Hence, a catch-22 situation.

What is more popular is a one-page plan which covers all of the components of the traditional business plan.

Some of the key areas this plan covers:
- Top 5 SWOT (Strengths, Weaknesses, Opportunities, and Threats)
- Your core values and beliefs
- Your Primary Mission
- Targets
- Goals
- Actions this quarter
- 90-Day Theme
- Key KPI's
- Key Indicators
- Financial Summary and Budgets

It's possible to get all of this on one sheet of paper!

Couple this with a 90 day cycle of plans so that you are breaking your goals into quarterly sprints, and you have an excellent way to manage your business at your fingertips.

A 90-day action plan would include the following elements:
- Your main focus
- Why, What, When and Who
- KPI's
- Financial Targets

It's possible to create this sort of plan in a Sunday afternoon and spend the next few months refining it.

Launch Ideas

As promised, we wanted to provide you with a few quick and easy launch ideas.

Let's start with why so many people choose the exact opposite!

The biggest challenge we see in the industry is a plethora of "strategies" originating from marketing gurus that sometimes show a very detailed and complicated approach.

The problem with a startup is they may not have a substantial list or an inexpensive way to reach their audience. This can lead to spending large sums of money on pay-per-click ads on Facebook or Google, with poor results or expensive conversion rates.

Here are the mistakes that we have seen many startups make, in our opinion...

1. They assume they know their potential buyer well and don't spend the time to get really clear on their audience
2. They create complex offers with multiple options - a confused mind never buys!
3. If they send enough traffic to a website, they assume it will eventually make money without considering the "temperature" of the visitor
4. They go low ticket price assuming that, if they can get thousands of customers, they will make good money, but this only works if your cost per sale is lower than the price set
5. They avoid having to sell one-on-one, assuming a well-written sales page will do the job without ever getting feedback from prospects
6. They assume that all they need to do is hire a great copywriter and it will solve all their problems
7. They try to do too much too soon, jumping between projects, searching for the holy grail

We could go on, but we think you get the point.

So, let's start again and give you our recipe for launches.

Before you even offer a product to a mass-market, you need to "beta" test it. If you look at the large corporations, they spend a lot of time and money on product development. While these large corporations have the infrastructure to support it, the challenge for smaller businesses is that this can be a long and expensive process—and not necessarily one that you will be able to afford.

The reality is that, if you can sell something to a hundred people, you can sell it to thousands of people—provided it's scalable. So, let's say you wanted to run a group coaching business and decided to charge $497 to join. But your biggest challenge is that you don't have any real list of buyers, and you no idea where to start.

Even worse, you don't really know your "best buyer".

So, here are a few ideas:
1. Launch a podcast talking about your potential buyer's problems. You will always get paid very well for solving problems.
2. Write a cheat sheet or checklist that solve problems or give good ideas and get people to signup to access it.
3. Create a survey to get ideas about what problems people have and provide a bonus for completing it.
4. Start a Facebook Group that focuses on the problem or solution and see if you can recruit like-minded people to join and contribute.
5. Start a small beta group—either free or paid—and have regular Q&A calls to educate and gain ideas about what they need, this forms part of a bigger launch once you have a viable product.

Once you have some ideas and framework from here you can then build a bigger offer and test that on the market. The focus here does not warrant large volumes of work. You want to find an easy and quick way forward.

Fast Market Research

The mistake that many new entrepreneurs make is trying to sell something no one wants to buy.

Many of these entrepreneurs operate with the idea that you target a broad audience based on their industry or other demographics that are vague, such as age or sex.

The broader you go, the worse it gets. Go too far and you'll end up as nothing to no one. For your business to bring in revenue, you need to be something to someone.

But first, you need to find out who that someone is.

What we are discussing next can easily be done in less than a day and will save you a lot of time and money in the end.

The first rule of marketing is that you should be able to describe your best customer so well that they think you must have been stalking them!

The first step is to discover what keywords your market uses. This can be accomplished in a few ways:

1. Google "Google Keyword Planner"
2. Use Google Insights
3. Search Amazon
4. Insert quotes on either side of a phrase and paste it into search.twitter.com. Look for tweets for those that are frustrated, would directly benefit, or are suggestive of a wish—ignore advertisers
5. Search Youtube
6. Setup Google alerts; signup for keywords
7. Do a Facebook search

Dedicate some time to researching your market by pasting your chosen subject into the search box to see what pops up in these platforms.

Create a spreadsheet of all of the posts and comments which seem to have the longest, most engaged or most passionate text.

Look for patterns—is there a contrarian position that might be suggested from your research?

At this stage, you are looking for the top 5-10% of relevant results so you can refine your spreadsheet to focus on what angles you might take in your marketing.

You are looking for one critical need that you could use to differentiate yourself from your competitors in the market.

In your research, look for "hyper-responsive text".

Even in your surveys, people who respond in detail are more likely to buy a product or service, because they are passionate about the problem or solution.

There are three questions you want to ask your ideal prospect or customer.

The WHAT question—e.g. "what is your single biggest question about…

"The Why question—e.g. "Why would that make a difference in your life?"

The HOW HARD question—e.g. How hard has it been for you to find a good answer about….?"

And just like that, you've filled out a fairly detailed profile of your best customer, and you can now work on being a better *something* for that *someone*.

The Buyers Journey

The buyer's journey is an important concept for any marketing strategy.

How are your potential buyers getting from stage one ("Do I even have a need?") to a fully-justified decision?

How can you, as a marketer, gain this knowledge to create marketing messages and concepts focused around the customer lifecycle?

It's possible that 70% of the new buyer's journey is complete before they even reach out to a supplier. Marketers need to adjust their strategies to cope with these changing consumer purchasing practices.

So, what can a marketer do about the 70% of the buyer's journey that they're missing out on? What are buyers doing during this time?

Let's start with Awareness

What is the buyer's need?

At the beginning of the potential buyer's journey, they are most likely to be aware of two things: your company, and whether they have a need. At this stage, buyers are wondering: "how do I know if I'm interested if I don't even know you exist?"

At this point, it's your job to create and build their awareness of you so that they begin to understand what you can do for them.

Your content and messaging should be focused on your buyer's real pain points—you shouldn't focus primarily on your product or brand.

Once your buyers begin to understand that they have a particular pain point, their research will start.

For up to 72% of potential buyers, they'll likely look to Google.

Their research begins with general search terms, as they start to explore their options. Buyers are on the lookout for educational material, customer reviews, and testimonials at this stage.

You need to make sure that these types of resources are readily available on your website or landing pages.

You should consider using a marketing automation tool so that you can start tracking the download of this information and collect prospect information at the same time.

While they aren't ready to hear your sales presentation, it's never too soon to start gathering some insight into your prospect's specific requirements.

Now, they proceed to further research; they'll begin to understand which requirements will and will not meet their needs, allowing them to order their questions during the demonstration.

At this point, buyers can begin to eliminate suppliers who don't provide the features or service that they want, fine-tuning their focus to just a few competing suppliers.

Making sure you have Educational or Informational content like white papers, analyst reports, and industry reports. This content is going very important at this point.

They will then move onto **Consideration Stage**.

The buyer has narrowed their choices down to just a few companies, and they'll return to the research stage again. Statistics show that 70% of buyers return to Google at least two to three times during the period of ongoing research, looking deeper into each company's specific offerings to see how they can solve their particular pain points.

Then at some point in their research phase, they will start to **Compare**.

At some stage, the prospective buyer will begin doing in-depth comparisons of each product or service that they are considering.

Before getting to decision time, they will need to justify their purchase. Therefore, you need to have solid reasons why they should choose your product over someone else's.

Now it's time to make a **Decision**. They'll start picturing what happens after the purchase—preparation, implementing setup costs, and what support they will need—then the final details will determine which product or service solution best fits their needs and budget.

As you can see, the best way to put your business on the buyer's map is to understand and support the Buyer's Journey; ultimately, the buyer's decision will be down to their perceived quality of the product or service, but you need to get your business to the final stage first, and that is why the Buyer's Journey is so important.

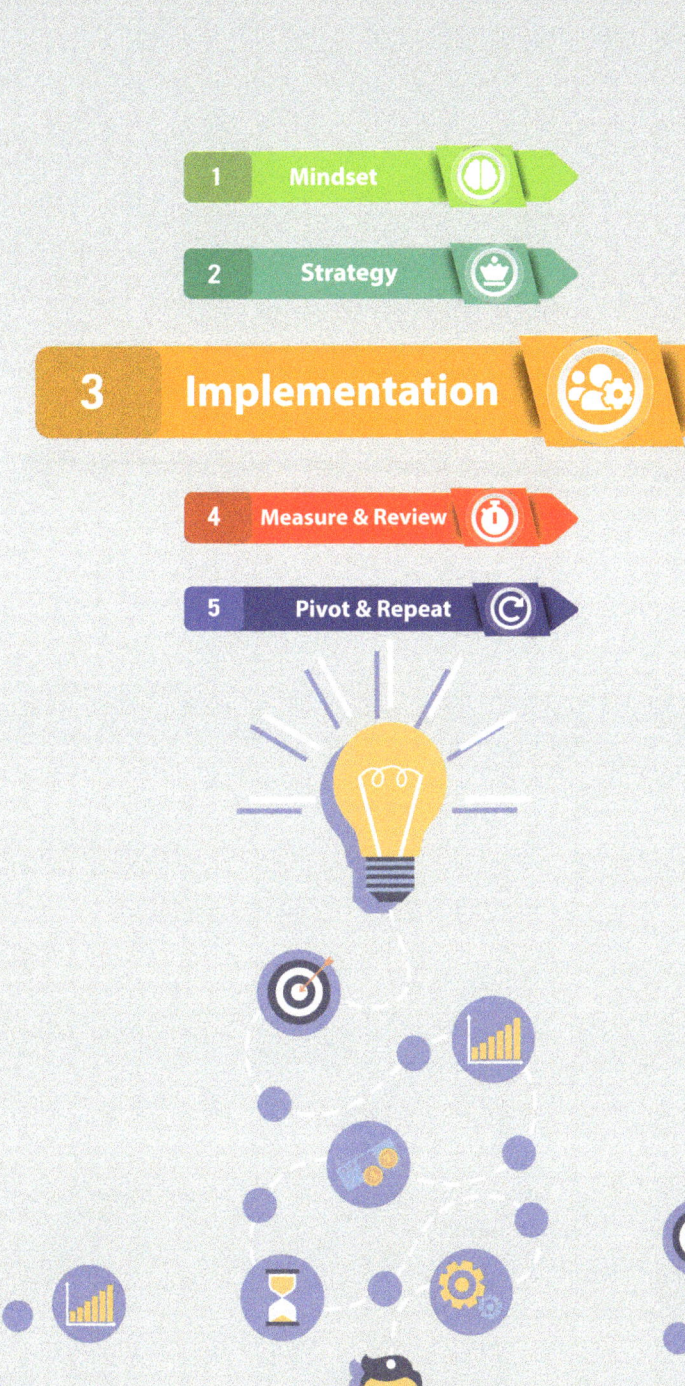

1. Mindset
2. Strategy
3. Implementation
4. Measure & Review
5. Pivot & Repeat

The New Online Business System

If you want to create a real growth-based sustainable business, our advice is to focus on building your own complete system; become independent from "Big Tech" so you can't be banned or throttled. Use them to send traffic to your own assets, like a website, recurring membership, online e-commerce shop, or e-learning platform and start building your own audience.

After thousands of hours of consulting and deploying marketing systems, the following is a blueprint for what we believe a typical online entrepreneur needs to be successful in today's highly-competitive marketplace:

Your major focus should be the overall customer experience. You will also want to try to be as frictionless as possible throughout. At the same time, employ as much automation as possible.

You should start with a mobile-ready website that tightly integrates your content-based assets, such as your podcast channel, on-demand videos, courses, memberships, and blogs.

At the same time, you will want to able to seamlessly build your subscriber database and automatically email them when new content is available.

You will need to design some pages to promote free checklists, blueprints, and/or ebooks to build your email list. You will want the ability for your visitors to buy your products/services and be able to handle the delivery of your digital download or physical product on the same site. At the same time, you may wish to upsell products at checkout. By segmenting your prospects, you can build powerful followup emails.

Your marketing module should trigger emails or actions based on your prospect's behavior, as well as help them progress through your courses and products.

You should have multiple payment gateways. This reduces the risk of one portal withholding funds if you grow too fast. You could also sell products in different currencies to lower buyer resistance.

You may want the ability to create a recurring membership system where you can charge users regularly, typically monthly or yearly, and allow them to easily update their records with you.

You may want different front-end websites, but you will want the eCommerce and backend accounts/member area to apply for all sites so you can manage it easily. This allows you to promote different angles of your business that all lead to the same place.

To grow your business, you should create an affiliate program and encourage referrers or affiliates to share your products and services for rewards.

At the end of the process, the prospect or customer should finish their initial journey in your back-end membership area, which includes all of their invoices, downloads, and bonus content. You don't want your customers fumbling around with separate websites looking for all this information! It's vital to have a ticketing system or similar integrated customer service system to support your customers.

The next step is to create a highly-engaged community for your clients and prospects that provides extra value behind a secure login and keeps them focused on you and coming back for your content.

To further engage users, you need to gamify your community through status badges and rewards systems.

Think about creating courses where your members can learn online at their own pace. Your course system should allow them to progress step-by-step as they do each lesson, not necessarily on a weekly release schedule where they could quickly get behind and give up. You should also encourage students to engage with other students.

What if they didn't need to download a worksheet PDF they never actually complete?

You need a system to allow them to leave their responses as they work through the lessons. This will give you the ability to see all of their answers, which means you also know where they are in the course.

3 Implementation

This means that no one is left behind!

A useful feature is to be able to assign a task to your students as they progress through the course. You could also create a coaching program based on their task list.

You also need a powerful analytics reporting system that tells you exactly where your traffic is coming from and what they're clicking on to help make decisions for your marketing campaigns.

You will also want a single dashboard to run your business, view statistics, create content, and manage your business.

Ideally, you should build a procedure system (Knowledge Base) so your staff and outsourcers can run your processes the same way every time. Make it easy to create step-by-step instructions rather than having to continually re-train staff.

What if you wanted to create a mastermind group?

It would be best if you could group people together and allow users to be able to access Q&A calls, group tasks, and results in a logical and centralised way.

It would also help to have a project management system to help you and your team manage your projects as well as client ones.

Most importantly, your platform needs to have fast loading times, or you risk driving customers away!

How long do you think it would take to implement all of this?

Maybe a year or longer!

We have spent thousands of dollars and many fruitless hours in search of the best all-in-one platform that has most of the features I wanted. But, even after all that, I could never find such a system. In frustration, I set out on a journey to develop my own unique platform, completely based around the needs of entrepreneurs, coaches, consultants, authors, podcasters, publishers, and mastermind groups.

We called it evolvepreneur.app. My mission is to start a revolution to help entrepreneurs establish their own complete business system to compete with the "big tech" end of town.

Don't become a cog in the machine; create your own machine.

I challenge you to focus on building your own complete business community platform.

Take control of your destiny and sleep better a night!

Websites, Landing Pages and Sales Pages

It doesn't matter WHAT you sell, you only need four types of webpages... MAXIMUM.

In fact, you might not even need them all!

These are the four basic webpages your business likely needs:

1. **Opt-in Page**. Any page where you collect someone's contact information falls into this category. This includes webinar registration pages, "squeeze pages", upsell pages, and funnels.
2. **Sales Page.** This could be a sales letter, a video sales letter, a page that shows a webinar (which is simply a longer version of a video sales letter).
3. **Content Page.** This is a page featuring content that attracts visitors to your website that addresses a problem that they are thinking about. This could be an article, a blog post, or a tutorial.
4. **Order Page.** Where people enter their payment information to pay for a product or service that you offer.

You may find that you don't require a Content Page, but it's a good thing to have to attract organic traffic to your site, and by extension, your products or services. Likewise, you may not need an Opt-in Page for your business to function and bring in revenue, but it's a good idea to build a few pages to extract that information from your customers (typically an email address) so you can create future opportunities to sell new products or services to old customers.

For example, if a customer buys a toilet brush from you today, they may also be interested in purchasing your newer, more advanced electric toilet brush months later. The only way they'll find out about your new product is through advertising on platforms not owned by you—TV, Google AdWords, YouTube, etc.—or, preferably, from an email that they have given you permission to send (i.e. they have opted in to receiving marketing emails).

Getting a customer is the hardest part, and recurring customers are the easiest and most reliable source of income for your business, so you need to hold on as tightly as you can to the people who have proven their interest in your products and services.

Don't let your customers escape so easily after buying just once from you!

Now, when it comes to your email campaigns ...there are only TWO types of email sequences you need.
1. **A Click Sequence**. This is where you're telling someone to go take a look at some information.
2. **A Countdown Sequence.** This is an offer that is going to expire soon.

Does that make you feel more in control?

If you can design your plans around these major categories, hopefully, you won't get lost in the weeds.

In the many years of designing online campaigns, it is very easy to end up with a complex web of pages for a single offer.

One of the reasons why we developed Evolvepreneur.app was to simplify this process.

By having a centralised back end system and common repeated processes, it means you can keep the volume of pages you need to a minimum.

The "tech stack" sometimes becomes a sort of badge of honour in the industry. This is how many applications, plugins and tools you use for running your business.

Today there is an "app for that" for almost any process you want to create. But how well does it all play together?

Here is a standard "tech stack" that you would see if someone had coaching or consulting business and wanted to support blogs, podcasts, and sell a membership plan:
- WordPress main site to handle blogs, podcasts, and the main pages for the business. Often, the theme you choose is complicated and you need a web developer to implement and manage it for you.
- Clickfunnels to handle the sales funnel side to support offers. This is sometimes this is done within WordPress with one of the various plugins you can obtain.

- A membership plugin or another solution like Kajabi so that the customer can use and progress through the course being sold.
- An e-Commerce plugin or 3rd party cart solution.
- A podcast host platform like Libsyn or BluBrry.
- A Contact management system or email campaign software.
- A customer support system such as a 3rd party ticket system to be able to help and communicate with customers that face issues (which they most certainly will).

That's not the end of it. If you want something beyond this basic system, you have to look into implementing multiple payment gateways and multiple currencies if you want to sell into different countries without having to rely on one payment solution.

So, before you venture into your business system, make sure you are going in with your eyes open. The more solutions you cobble together, the harder it is to set up and maintain.

When we designed evolvepreneur.app, we built in all the necessary modules, such as blogs, podcasts, e-Commerce, e-Learning, surveys, customer support, and the knowledge base for both internal company use and for pointing customers to when they need help for a process that is well-documented.

To setup your business system with evolvepreneur.app, the process might look like this, taking you about an afternoon to achieve:

1. Create the products you want to sell and set up the payment gateways and currencies you want to use.
2. Create your front-facing pages and link any products and upsells to the pages
3. Setup your Blog Homepage and schedule your blog posts, then connect a subscription button
4. Setup your Podcast Show Page and prepare/schedule your episodes, then connect a subscription button
5. Create your course and lessons and link any courses to your products
6. Create your surveys and link any products or offers
7. Use Zapier to connect to a CRM or Email Campaign System
8. Setup your Support Department so you can handle any support issues

This basic business system can be fully implemented quickly with evolvepreneur.app, and facilities like thank you pages and customer access to downloads or courses are automatically handled.

Additionally, one of the best tools you can use is a mockup application.

There are a lot of these tools around, such as Mockflow, which is what we use.

This tool allows you to create the basic design of the website or landing pages and insert any text and even images. Using these tools can make it far easier to give to your designer.

At the same time, it gives you a way to visualise the final outcome.

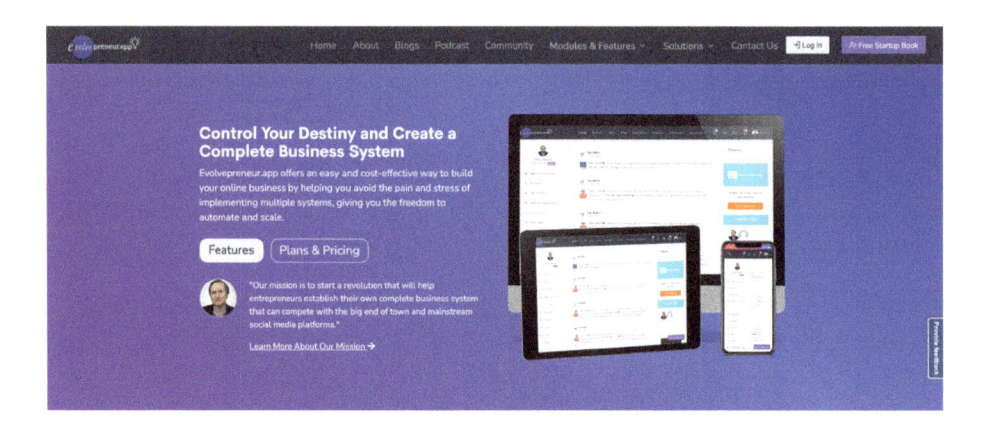

Podcasting

When we speak to entrepreneurs, they often say that creating a podcast show is on their bucket list. But, contrary to their expectations, creating a podcast show isn't as difficult as it seems.

In fact, creating a podcast show is actually one of our lazy marketing strategies.

If you want to set up an audio-only podcast, it can be done in a few hours; it isn't a complex project.

Podcasts are predominantly distributed through something called an RSS feed, which is a page written in XML that holds various data and metadata necessary to distribute your podcast. This often stops the new podcaster in their tracks and is typically the main reason why they put off the idea of starting a podcast for so long.

We think this is actually a little ironic, as RSS stands for Really Simple Syndication—it's meant to make your life easier, not harder!

This feed is typically created by the hosting platform, although we believe you should own your feed. More on that later.

Practically, it's just a link that looks like this: https://evolvepreneur.club/feed/podcast

If you look closely at the page this link directs to in a web browser like Google Chrome or Mozilla Firefox, it will quickly start to make some sense. You can see the show details, followed by links to and details about the episodes.

The truth is, podcast platforms like Apple Podcasts (the biggest platform on the market currently) don't actually host anything; descriptions, episodes, and show artwork are taken from RSS feeds like this. They simply hook into this feed, which is updated every time you make changes on your hosting platform—which, in our case, is Evolvepreneur, a fully-featured podcasting solution.

Once they acquire the information they need, they stream it on-demand via their website, or in the case of Apple Podcasts, their app.

RSS feeds, over 20 years old at the time of writing, are a truly amazing and simple tool that can be and are also used for blogs in a similar manner.

If you decide that you don't like an episode that you've already produced and pushed to the RSS feed, all you need to do is delete it from the feed, and it's gone forever.

The best part is that you don't have to learn XML to create and manage an RSS feed; all podcast hosting platforms worth their salt will automatically generate an RSS feed and update it whenever you push changes on the platform. You simply need to take the resulting link to the RSS feed and plug it into a podcasting platform like Apple Podcasts.

That's it! You're done! This is the hardest aspect of podcasting to get your head around, but fortunately, you don't even need to know any of the technical specifics to know how to use an RSS feed.

Don't think you have to do a daily or weekly show. Try to get 3-5 episodes done and schedule them out to release each week at the same time. Now you are 3-5 weeks ahead of the latest episode and can record in bulk to keep to the schedule.

To get your podcast up and running, you need the following components:
1. Strategy around what the show is called and what it's about. Work out a content plan and consider getting some guests to come on the show.
2. Hosting Platform for your show's metadata (such as title, description, author name, etc.) and audio files for episodes.
3. Show art for your cover.
4. A decent microphone (the Blue Yeti is a popular beginner choice that is easy to setup and use).
5. Audio editing tools and that patience to learn how to do it, or someone who can do this for you.
6. A strategy to get email subscribers listening to your show.

The process works like this:
1. Setup your podcast platform with all the necessary information, such as show title, categories and description, and generate your RSS feed

URL (as discussed above, it's a news feed that provides platforms with the necessary details to host your show and stream your episodes).
2. Record and edit your episodes .
3. Upload and schedule your finalized episodes.
4. Signup for Apple Podcasts, the biggest podcasting platform, and start listing your show on other platforms afterward.
5. Officially launch your show and post your episodes on social media and in email lists as they release to build up subscribers.

After podcasting for over 7 years, we have learned that there are several key things that you need for a podcast show.

This includes:
- Awesome Podcast Show Page
- Great Show Art with strong branding
- **Own Your RSS Feed**—this is a vitally important freedom that you don't want to give up. You should have your own RSS Feed using your own domain. If you use many of the popular platforms, they will lock you into using their domain name for your RSS feed. What this means is that you are renting the feed that is used to send the episodes to the various platform distribution sites, such as Apple Podcasts. With our platform, you own your RSS Feed. This is a fundamental mistake that most Podcasters make, and it can be a nightmare to fix.
- Strategic Advice and professional setup
- The extra bits that make a massive difference
- Upsell products straight off your Show and Episode Page
- You can have a video on the podcast page as well, providing extra value
- Ability to have email subscribers and alert them automatically when a new episode comes out. Almost no one does this, and if they do, they never give you the email addresses.
- This means you can create a community around your show and they can go into the backend of the website and see what you have to offer.
- Create a membership (free or paid)
- Sell Courses and Memberships to grow your revenue
- Build a Community
- Track your statistics to help grow your show
- Get Expert advice whenever you need it

- **Guest Host System**—we make it easy for you to manage guests for your show. We even have a system for them to apply to be on your show and then work through a process before the interview. Guest Hosts will have their own profile page. If you aren't using Evolvepreneur for your podcasting, you will need to set this up using another system like WordPress

The Evolvepreneur platform fulfils all of these needs, and if the system had been around 7 years ago, we would have used it to launch and manage our podcast.

Evolvepreneur Podcast Packages

How Does it Work?

Our Podcast Show packages are designed to help guide you through the entire process and be there for you after the setup.

There are several phases:

Phase 1 - Strategic Advice—Your Success Manager will spend 60 minutes with you to make sure your ideas and concepts are strategically aligned. It's great to have an expert sounding board before you dive in.

Phase 2 - Setup & Design—The setup phase where we will design your show page and artwork and create your show pages. Your Success Manager will spend 60 minutes with you to create the best designs for your podcast.

Phase 3 - Create Your Episodes—Now it's your turn! We have a Podcast Host Course to guide you through all the technical and art of the podcast. You can also ask our Expert Support Team any questions along the way. If you need your episodes edited, we can also arrange for this as an additional service.

Phase 4 - Launch and Grow—By now, you have created your initial episodes and ready to launch. Our expert team will help get your ready to launch the show.

Phase 5 - Revenue!—If you take the "Done For You Package", Your Success Manager will spend 60 minutes discussing the best ways to leverage the platform to earn revenues. Our goal is to find a way to go from $0 to $5,000 a month recurring revenue using your show as the conversation starter.

Your Own Show

What do we mean by "your own show"?

When entrepreneurs start out promoting their business, they typically run ads or social media posts that are random and inconsistent. There's no overall strategy involved.

When you look at any very successful person, they often have a TV or Radio Show. What we are suggesting is that we backward engineer this concept.

If you created your own "show", it would not only allow you to formalise your content logically and sequentially; it would also give your future customers a closer connection to you.

In the world of marketing, there are 2 very different main marketing strategies.
- **Spray and Pray**—where huge volumes of posts, videos, blogs and other content is created and published.
- **Narrow and Deep**—create less content but narrowly focused and comprehensive in detail.

Let's dig into the Narrow and Deep. If you did your initial research well enough, you will have a good idea of your ideal prospect and buyer.

By going deep into your topic, your content is going to stand out.

At this stage, you don't want to over-think this concept of a show.

In reality, this could also be your podcast. If you are not confident on video, start with audio.

If you are going to have guests, try to get both video and audio, and if the video doesn't work out, it doesn't matter, because you only planned for audio anyway.

But sometimes, you can re-purpose portions of your video for promotional purposes.

The mistake a lot of entrepreneurs make at this stage is to try to create, produce, and promote all at once.

This quickly becomes confusing and often results in some steps not getting the attention they need.

So, we are suggesting this plan:

1. Spend a few days on creating the concept and strategies for your show. Plan on a "season" of 12-13 episodes at a rate of one per week. That means you could, in theory, have 3-4 seasons a year.
2. Produce your episodes. If you are pre-recording, it will be a lot easier than going live on Facebook. You may consider doing a live show but bear in mind that both platforms can premiere or essentially fake a live show. This takes the pressure off, especially in the early days, when you aren't yet a confident, veteran podcaster.
3. At the promotion stage, you should have scheduled your content and can start to prepare your marketing materials. For example, creating short outtakes of 1-2 minutes.

You need to consider where your primary show platform is. For example, if it's a podcast, you may restrict the show to appearing on your podcast platform, eg. iTunes. For Youtube, drive traffic to that video.

So, be clear on your goals, each platform has its own approach. It's a bit like choosing a TV channel and sticking to it.

Repurpose your content. For example, transcribe your episode and make it a blog post. Maybe create a LinkedIn Article, etc. and include the text on the actual show itself. Your goal here should be to build email subscribers, offering bonus materials for them to signup.

Level Up Ideas

One of the best ways to promote engagement is to hold a Q&A mini-show every so often, covering feedback and questions the main show content has highlighted. This is on-the-fly content creation during your promotion stage that is designed to encourage some live interaction with your viewers.

Create a free membership club where when they subscribe and get extra bonuses and content from you.

Get guest appearances on other podcast shows so you can cross-promote yourself.

Create some front-end surveys to gain insight into your subscribers.

3 Implementation

Evolvepreneur.app lets you achieve all the above with ease.

We have a complete podcast show platform solution as well as an On-Demand Video System. You also have a blog home page. It is very easy to add a subscribe button on these show or home pages and we can deliver their free content or membership system.

At the same time, our system automatically alerts your subscribers when new episodes come out. You want them on your platform first so you can control the traffic.

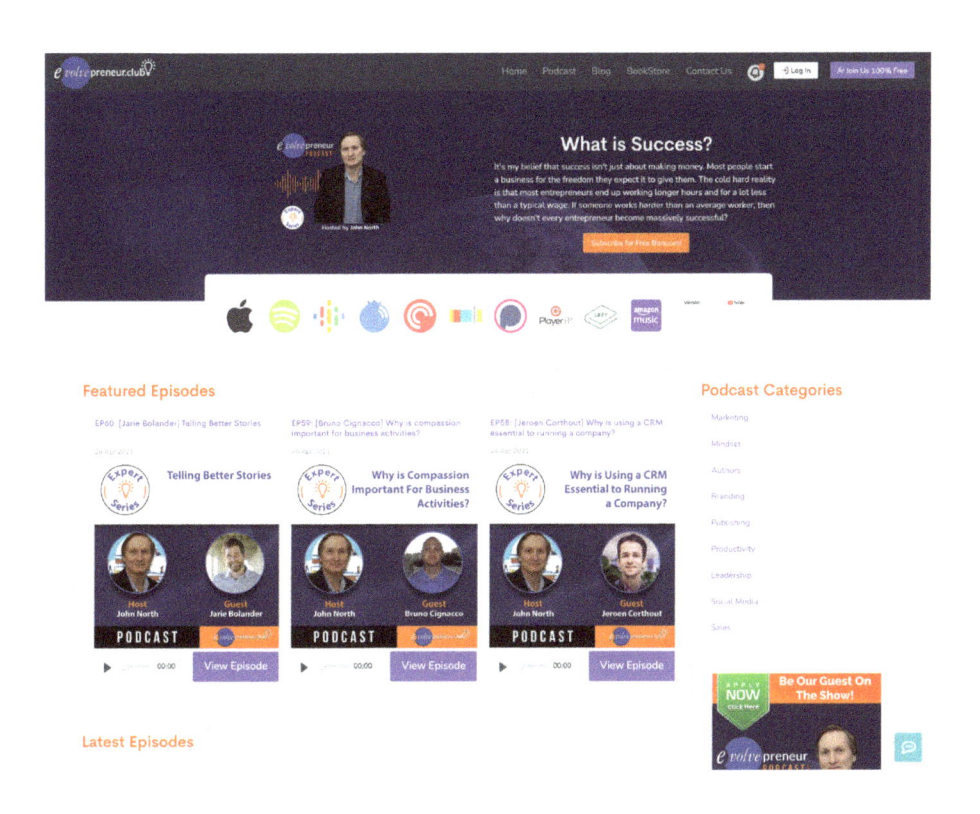

Building Subscribers

You need to own your own stuff!

It's all very well to amass social media followers on Twitter and Facebook, but you don't own them. You don't have their contact details. You can't contact them outside of that platform. You can't send a marketing email to them because you don't know their email address. And even on the platform itself, the situation isn't ideal. These platforms are making it harder for you to interact with your followers without payment all the time.

And worse yet, all of these platforms can ban you in an instant with no way to recover the followers you've spent all that time amassing.

But that's not to say that social media isn't worth investing in. It most certainly is, but you shouldn't let the relationship begin and end there.

Your goal should be to leverage these platforms to get followers onto your email list.

This strategy gives you control over your destiny and extends your ability to reach your list any time you need to.

Your podcast show is another area where you should be converting subscribers to customers.

Remember, you need to slowly build a connection with your prospects through your podcast show. This will give you a bit of celebrity status and will certainly enable you to command higher prices for your services.

For this reason, having a subscriber strategy is essential.

This is where your customer journey comes into play. Once they feel they know you, it's time to start to move them through your pre-determined pathway.

In the early days, you might simply have them book a call with you to start a conversation.

This is especially handy where you can use surveys to help qualify your prospects before a call.

The rule of thumb is that each email address is worth $1 per month to you.

So, consider using a low ticket offer to convert initial subscribers to some value to cover your marketing costs.

If someone spends some money with you, they are likely to spend more later.

Could you have a $10 per month membership offer?

Recurring revenue is the most powerful way to make money and keep making money.

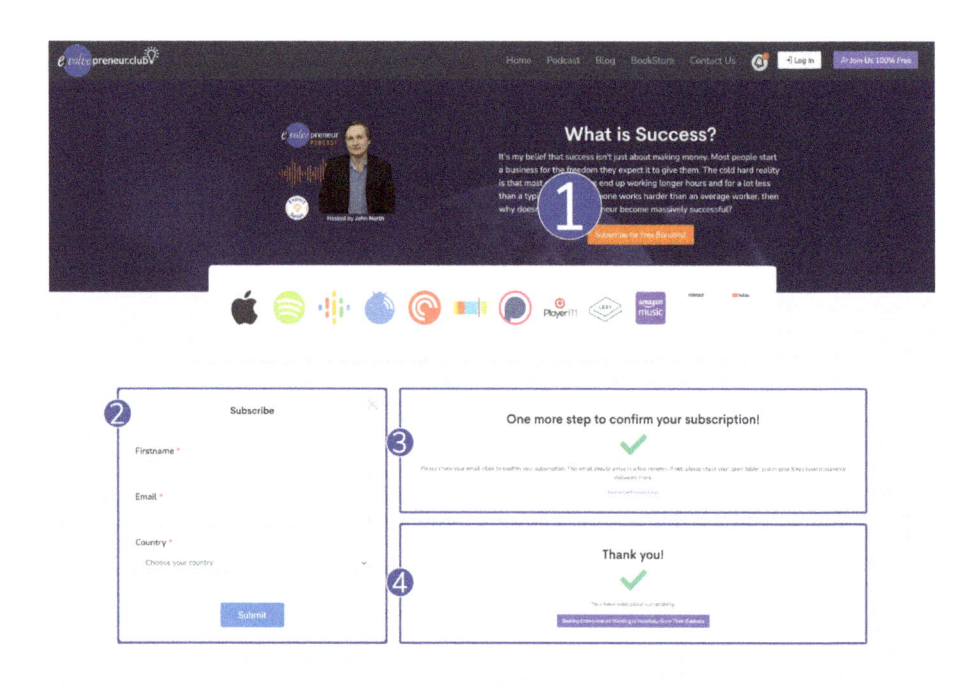

Memberships and Recurring Income

"Twenty years from now you will be more disappointed by the things that you didn't do than by the ones you did do. So throw off the bowlines. Sail away from the safe harbour. Catch the trade winds in your sails. Explore. Dream. Discover."

—Mark Twain

If you were smart about your original goals, you would have thought about what your business would look like when it's done.

The reality is, the day you're hired is the day your fired... it's just a matter of when.

Many entrepreneurs will try to sell their business when a disaster strikes. Maybe they are sick or having cash flow issues.

If you plan to sell your business eventually, start building your business for sale in the first place. This means putting in training and procedures manuals and staff in place.

A business built for sale will look very different from one built off a great idea or a lifestyle business.

However, some businesses are unsaleable for lots of reasons. With these types of businesses, you need to focus on recurring income—some way that you can earn revenue for limited or no ongoing involvement.

As part of our strategy, we have promoted a product that pays 40% weekly of the recurring income they make.

Most weeks, we get paid between $500 and $900. Over the past year, that has accounted for over $22,000 in revenue for virtually no work on our side!

It's enough for us to hire an extra employee for free. Even if we stopped working, that money will still flow in.

Think about whether you could sell off chunks of your business. We have someone who operates part of our services and we receive 25% of the revenue. We help with marketing and tech, but it isn't a heavy commitment for us.

You could license your idea and create a course for people to duplicate your results.

You could create a legacy business for your children. This is part of our plan. These businesses are ready-made machines for them.

Aim to work on your business, not in it.

Starting with a strategy of how you can build memberships that rebill every month or year is essential to any viable business. Predictable revenue buys freedom—the very reason why most entrepreneurs start a business.

These strategies will get you through the bad times in cashflow. The recent pandemic shows the real reason why you need a solid foundation of recurring revenue.

Big-ticket products are great for initial cash flow, but usually take longer to sell and cost to generate.

Having a backup option for big-ticket is a great way to downsell and still convert sales.

However, you should be careful with designing your membership and offers. It's not common for an entrepreneur to create a complex pricelist of offers.

The most successful businesses have low numbers of products. For some time, Apple only had a small range of products. In recent years, they have introduced a large range of options, but if you look at their core range, these so-called products are really just option tweaking.

Our suggestion is to try to restrict yourself to no more than 5 products initially.

If you have a membership solution, consider 3 levels. People do love choice, but they don't like complexity.

Each level should be tailored towards a specific type of customer.

Success Journeys

What is a success journey, exactly?

We discovered the concept of "success paths" from Stu Mclaren from Tribe Workshop a few years ago. Stu created a WordPress plugin called "Wish List Member" and had thousands of users creating membership courses.

We have applied this concept not only in creating courses but also in writing books. It's most likely useful in other areas as well.

The idea is that your customer goes through a series of steps or pathways that leads to their eventual success.

The Success Journey is a concept designed to streamline people's thought processes and help them to move forward and make progress.

Create a document with a few headings. Across the top, you want 3-7 columns, and in each column, you put in the achievements and action steps a person at that point would need to take. Your Customer Success Path or Journey starts with the worst-case scenario, of where someone would start, and ends with the best-case plan of where they want to be.

Fill in the remaining stages with the big moments that will occur in between the two.

You will want to make sure that you have chosen names for those stages, that are positive and empowering.

For the characteristics, list or describe the traits of someone at every stage. What does someone at this stage think, feel, or do?

We recommend that you stay between three and seven stages. If you have less than three stages, there's simply not that much progression that could be life-changing for someone. If you have more than seven stages, people are going to get seriously overwhelmed, and that defeats the purpose of the success journey.

The Success Journey is crafted to help streamline people's thinking and to provide clarity in terms of them being able to get clear in terms of where they are and, specifically, what they need to do to move forward and make progress.

That's why prospects are coming to you. They have some problem or challenge in their life, and they're looking to be able to make progress toward resolving that problem or challenge and/or mastering a set of skills. But if you have no easy way of being able to identify that they're even making progress, that becomes a problem.

The other big benefit of this is it sifts and sorts through all of the information and helps your audience get crystal clear on the few things that are most relevant to them right now.

This is a very powerful concept that is worth spending time to master.

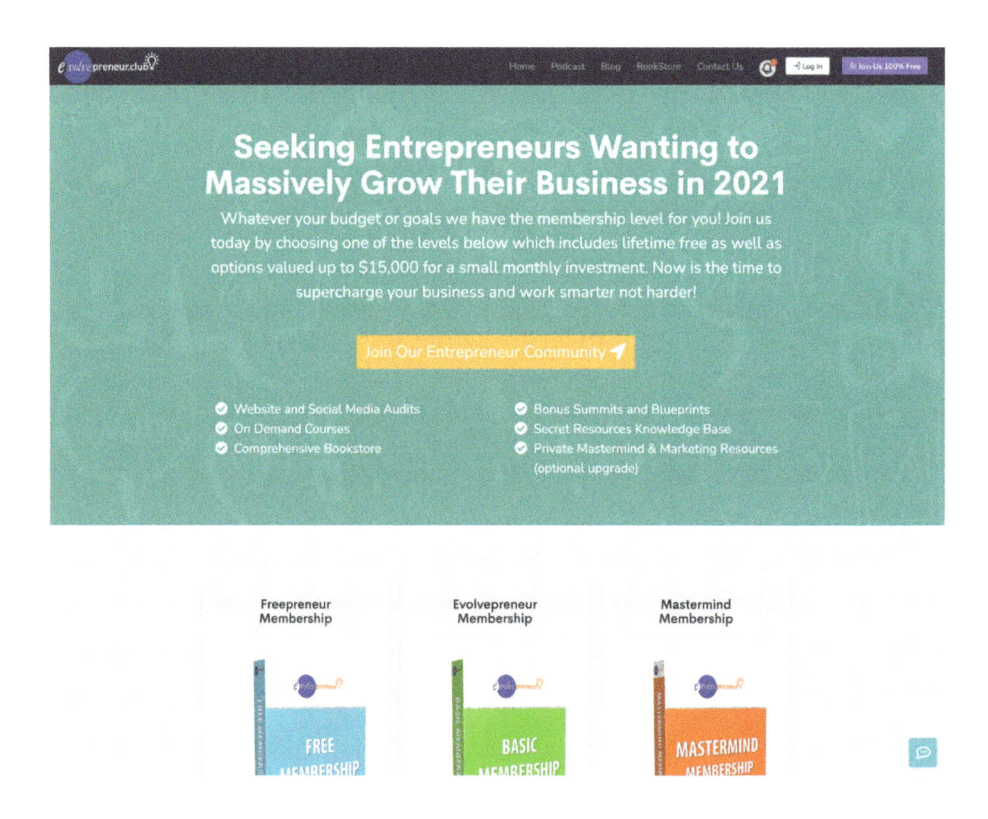

Surveys for Success

Surveys are one of the best ways to engage with your best buyers.

People will fill out a survey when they see something in it for them.

If you are just starting out, the best survey is called a "deep dive". The ASK Method® by Ryan Levesque goes into a lot of detail about these types of surveys.

The concept is that you ask a couple of questions like this:
1. When it comes to... what's the single biggest challenge you've been struggling with? (Please be as detailed and specific as possible)
2. Which of these best describes your team of employees at the moment?
3. What is your yearly gross revenue?
4. If we were to create a paid program on one of the following topics (and you had to choose just one), which of the following are you most interested in, and would've signed up for if already available?

What you are trying to do is get the hyper-responsive replies.

The ones that write a lot in question 1 above, specifically. These prospects are interested and have issues they may be prepared to pay you to resolve.

The next stage is to look at surveys that lead to defined outcomes.

For example, if you have decided your perfect customer needs at least 10 employees and One Million in turnover, you might create a survey that asks these questions, and based on their response, take them to a different outcome page.

Some people might be able to afford one-on-one help, while others might prefer a mastermind group option.

Given the massive power of surveys, the evolvepreneur.app system has a built-in ability to create basic or advanced surveys. For example, you can create a score-based survey that takes the prospects to different outcome pages based on their responses.

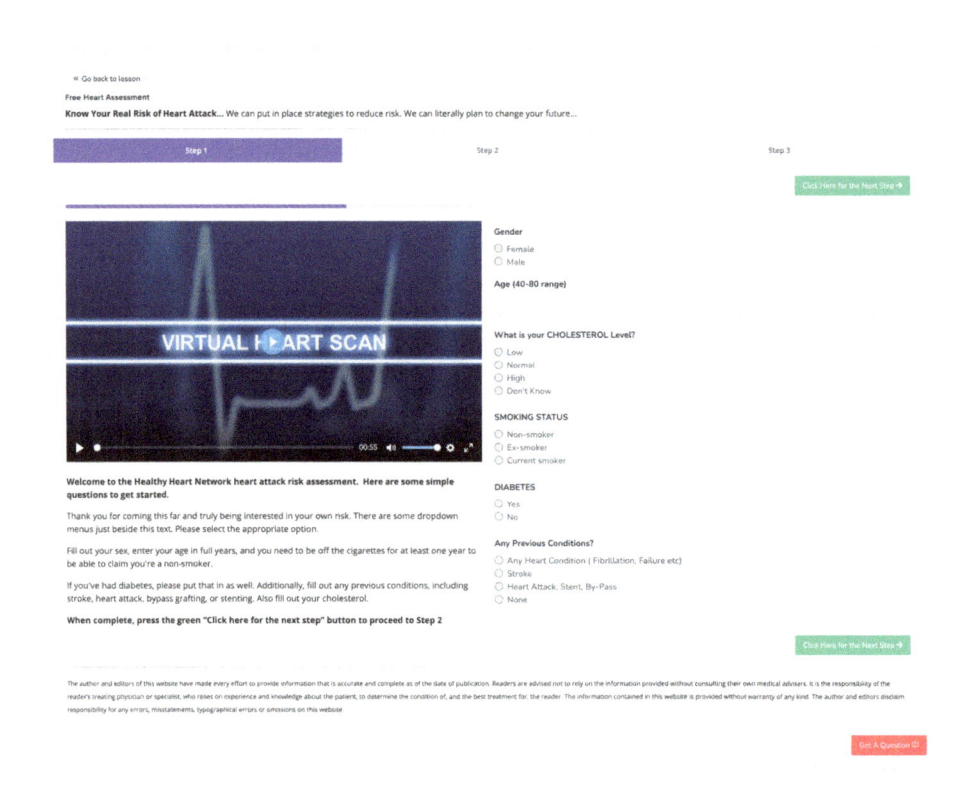

Courses and Masterminds

The online internet market has numerous gurus, each with their own advice on the best way to create a course or mastermind.

It is a great way to deliver quality products to your market. Masterminds can be a very powerful system to start with because you can build something live through Q&A and training calls and then convert it to a course later and automate it.

The challenge with either of these ideas can be complexity and perfection. It often paralyses the entrepreneur who wants to make their first attempt perfect.

This can lead to never actually launching and your ideas never seeing the light of day.

Here is a quick start idea…

Create a landing page that offers approved applicants access to a small beta group. This could be a paid program, or you could even offer it free to the right person.

Come up with a basic 3-4 week mastermind, perhaps with weekly calls and homework.

Using the power of surveys, take applications and approve the ones you think would fit.

The pressure of having to deliver content and a course will get you past perfection very quickly, and the expectation from your members is that it's a beta, so they are going to be less demanding when things go wrong.

Believe me, they will!

Remember not to over complicate this idea. Keep it simple and focus on one key solution; don't overwhelm your students.

Using evolvepreneur.app, you can complete this whole process—from creating the landing page, initial survey for application, eCommerce checkout, to the actual course work. Once you have created your course, you can plug in your calls and create surveys inside the lessons for your students to do the activities. It's all online without the need for downloading a workbook!

We have been able to build this whole process out in less than a day.

Now that's rapid implementation, right?

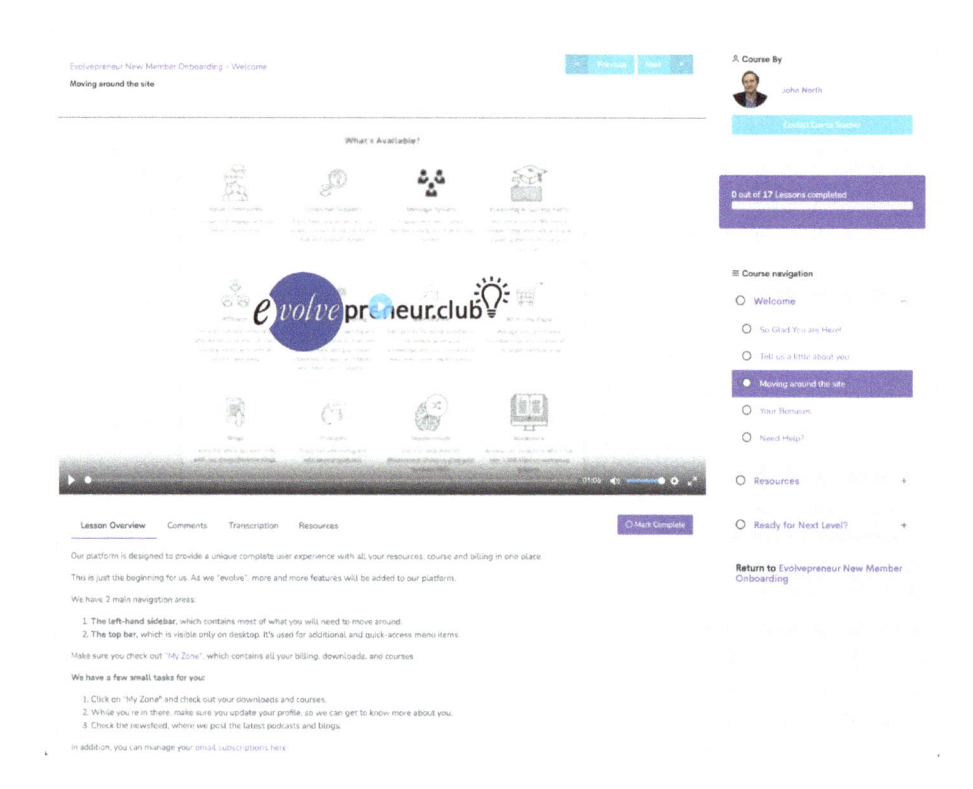

Good Project Management is Vital!

One of the most significant areas of focus for successful businesses is managing your overall projects and associated tasks, as well as your customers, staff and contractors in an efficient way.

Recent project management statistics show that 35% of project managers are still using spreadsheets to build resource plans. This means that your offline projects are not in real-time and relevant decision making is much slower than an online collaborative system.

Our mission for Evolvepreneur.app is to help empower Coaches and Consultants to create a solid business.

Below is how we can help and even if you don't use our platform gives you a framework to start with.

Here's What Our Project Management Module Can Do For You!

Evolvepreneur.app helps you keep everything together about your next project in one central place including files, discussions, tasks, which helps you avoid unnecessary duplication into 3rd party systems.

You can even create a template project and re-use it quickly for the next one.
- Save Time
- Afford expensive mistakes and cost overruns
- Transparent and real-time collaboration with your workers and customers

Tasks

Create Tasks to track each stage of a project, with the ability to mark items as complete and see at a glance how much is outstanding.
- You can assign a task to one or more individuals.
- They will receive emails to alert them about the task due.
- Assign tasks separately or as part of a project

- Assign Task Managers
- Set Deadlines
- Attach files
- Set and change Priorities
- Create a Task Template for quick re-use again

Task Owners

Typically a "Task Owner" is your customer who you have assigned to a project or task. This can also be you for internal tasks. They can see the tasks including any that are assigned to them. They can also comment and collaborate with you and your workers in real-time.

Task Workers

This category is designed for your staff or contractors to work on a task and optionally keep track of their time. The concept here is that you can leverage your workforce to do the work for your customers without necessarily having to manage every aspect.

You are also making them responsible in real-time for the project and it's success. Workers can submit their time logs for timesheet approval and payment as well.

If you are charging by the hour you can also engage the customer in keeping their payments to you on time and easily top up their points from their dashboard.

Time Billing

Many Projects are directly related to time, this can be a major area that entrepreneurs can lose money and be unable to recover the lost time afterward.

By logging your time and your workers/contractors you are generating a real-time track of the time spent.

At the same time, your customer knows the costs and time and can make adjustments and communicate with your team before the project goes sideways!

Billing Points

Whilst you can simply charge per hour, we have also added an innovative way to "gamify" your projects. We call it "billing points" where you create a department and assign to your workers. But at the same time, you can allocate a number of points per hour per type of work.

So for example admin work may attract 1 point per hour, but perhaps complex graphic design work is 2 points and your personal coaching is 3 points. Then all you need to do is connect an e-commerce product to the project system and set a price per point. This strategy has significant benefits including more revenues to better managed and happy workers to happier clients.

Comments

Our comment system allows you to provide feedback on the task and keep all the relevant parties in the communication loop with email notifications.

Attachments

Sometimes a picture is worth a thousand words! Simply attach any relevant documents and screenshots for your task so that everyone is in the loop.

Time Tracker

You and your workers can log time against tasks, tracked automatically with a start & stop timer. At the same time any logged billable time can reduce your customers' points balance.

TimeSheet Processing and Payments

One of the biggest challenges you will face when engaging workers to bill for their time is making sure the customer also gets charged.

Because the worker is logging their time against your customer project they are also generating the billing for that customer as well. At the end of the week for example the worker can "rollup" their time logs and submit to the TimeSheet Manager for approval who can then send it to the TimeSheet Accounts Manager for payment.

This system holds everyone accountable to the project and financial aspects.

Knowledge Base / Procedures / SOPs

Documenting your processes and procedures is often missed by entrepreneurs who then have to re-train staff when the previous employee moves on. In our system, you can create articles for every procedure and process in your business and then attach them to tasks.

Used in conjunction with the Project or Task template you have created a powerful turnkey business model.

Links to Ticket System

Our Project system lets you link your Project or Task to a customer ticket. This is an excellent way to handle workflow with your customers. They could create a ticket for task to be done and your workers can create or link tasks to the ticket.

This process means you can separate the task system from the end customer to avoid any issues.

User "less" System

This is our own term, what we mean is that we don't charge "per user" like almost every other project management system around. The project management system is a module and you can have as many users as you want in your own platform.

Of course, there are limitations around file storage but this is based on your overall hosting plan. Paying per user can be a very costly "tax" on success that we simply don't want be involved in!

Coaching and Consulting

One of the fastest ways to start a business is providing coaching or consulting services. It allows you to leverage your knowledge and experience and doesn't have a lot of overheads.

Be warned in our experience people never charge enough for their services.

Whilst it's a good idea to start low or free to get some initial clients, always raise your prices as you go to ensure you are well paid for your time.

At the same we find that these services are not always structured or automated to give their client a good experience and allow you to easily scale.

Our mission for Evolvepreneur.app is to help empower Coaches and Consultants to create a solid business.

Below is how we can help and even if you don't use our platform gives you a framework to start with.

Here's What The Evolvepreneur.app Coaching and Consulting Module Can Do!

Easy Billing and Onboarding

The most important first step to gaining a new client is actually getting paid. We make it easy via our e-Commerce system to create various service-based products and allow your customers to purchase these in their local currency (depending on the currencies you set of course).

At the same time, you can set up your "Post Purchase" which can be various automated processes that typically done manually.

Project Management

One of the most challenging aspects of coaching or consulting is managing client expectations and delivering on your promises. Coupled with our

Project Management Module, you can create tasks and even track your time or workers time to deliver your services.

Courses & Surveys

One of the most powerful ways to over-deliver to your clients is by providing them with an easy on-demand "blueprint". If you create a course a little like a Project you can have a step by step process for them to follow.

Add surveys into the lessons and they can give you immediate feedback and set the pre-work for your calls with them. Include videos and resources and your client is off and running as soon as they finish the checkout!

Knowledge Base

The Knowledge Base module has 2 key functions. You can allow your members to access various articles which could be simple help or even extending your knowledge.

The second way is to create a private "Staff Only" procedures and systems area.

- Create/Edit Articles
- Knowledge Base Categories
- Featured Articles
- Restrict Category access by Group
- Approval
- Process
- Enable/Disable Articles
- Link a product or custom link
- Videos and Images

Support Tickets

This is a great way to manage a client when you have a lot of details to share between you and them. Also you can have separate tickets for each aspect of your project or link them to the Project Management Module. The client simply can respond via email to any request and we will automatically import it.

Opportunities

As part of our CRM module you can track your future opportunities and track the success of your marketing.

Affiliate or Referrers

Most likely you get a lot of your new clients from referral and you should leverage these as much as possible.

Each of your clients are automatically assigned an unique code they can use to promote or refer you and this means when you get a new client they will be assigned as the referrer.

If you want to reward them with commission we make that easy to track as well!

Affiliates and Referral Partners

If you are looking to grow your business, one way is to seek help from others. These methods can be low cost because you don't usually pay unless you get a result.

But to get this right, you need to put yourself in their shoes.

It isn't uncommon to offer someone a 10% commission on a sale, for example. But your referral partner might not think that it's worth their while.

If you want to generate business this way, there are a couple of paths. Some business's entire strategy is to use referral partners and build their margins and marketing around it.

1. Offer referral commissions to your existing customers when they send new prospects your way. Be prepared to give them a decent amount and make a big deal of it when a prospect is received. Let them know the progress and outcome. Encourage them to send more and keep in touch. Send them additional gifts to show your appreciation.

2. Build a proper referral network. This approach takes more time and you need to be prepared to find referrers that will speak to you once a week, fortnight or month. The concept here is that they are almost treated like an employee or business partner. You want to spend time educating them about your solutions and teach them what sort of prospects you want. If they don't want to spend that amount of time with you, then it's likely they will never really be that useful as a referral base.

3. Resellers - this is a great way to build a business but requires a good system and reasonable margins. You need to provide all the tools and systems for them to be successful.

If you plan to have others share in your sales revenue, it's wise to build that into your pricing from day one. You need to consider that building strong relationships is vital to success, and time and resources need to be allocated to this.

Would a powerful referral system that increases your "bottom line" by 5-20% or more help improve your business?

Making more money is always the goal of every business, yet most business owners leave tremendous sums of money on the table by not having dynamic referral systems in place that excite their customers enough to recommend their business to others.

Once you have such systems set up, all it takes is a follow-up by yourself and your employees. Creating a referral system that rewards your employees and customers is not only possible but simple once you have your system in place.

Making sure your employees are on board with the plan and trained to use it is important if you truly desire to get referrals on a steady basis.

A **Dynamic Referral System** can produce a majority of your customers. Your customers don't want to and won't waste their time conducting research to decide which business to buy from.

Consider your own shopping habits. When was the last time you spent hours trying to find a new car repair mechanic, grocery store or restaurant?

Because most people find it difficult to make choices about even mundane things like shopping or restaurants, they would prefer that someone they know gives them a suggestion or referral.

This process removes the stress from their decision about where they should shop. Most people love trying new places after receiving positive recommendations from friends or associates.

They feel that if Sue or Joe says the place is good, they'll have a positive experience as well. Do you realize it's 500-1,000% more costly to use other advertising methods to bring customers to your door than to get just ONE referral?

Many businesses spend 15% or more of their total revenue on their advertising budgets…yet their referral customer base is twice that of the clients who come to them through paid advertising! With the hundreds of categories of referral programs available, we can focus our attention on two that are proven and tested, have a successful track record, take very little time to implement, and require little to no money or personal risk to put into action.

There are several types of Referral Systems:

3 Implementation

1. **The "Static" Referral System** - your customers are informed of your referral program and understand the "perks" they will receive from sharing information about your business with family, friends, associates, and anyone they meet who shows an interest in your service.
2. **The "Proactive" Referral System** - in this system, you will be directing the entire process that gives you the power to reach potential customers who have been influenced by their friends or associates.

They're prospects who, under normal circumstances, would never have heard of you or your business. You're motivating your customers to become "promoters" of your business or service by enticing them to share information about what you do with anyone and everyone they know.

System #1 - The "Static" Referral System

Every business can thrive by creating ways to get referrals. Referrals come from happy, satisfied clients who let others know about your service or products. And when the system is working well, those satisfied clients tell others about your business.

This typically happens by sheer luck if you don't have a systematic process in place. Your referrals will simply dribble in, hit and miss. Even a static referral system is better than none.

Otherwise, you'd be missing out on many new customers and the additional cash flow they produce. That "static" referral model calls for you and your employees to consistently ask for the names of all your client's friends, family, business associates and others who may need what you're offering.

Naturally, this can be done face-to-face, by email, or by letter. The key is the follow-up; it doesn't matter so much how you follow up.

The "static" model is only successful if your employees continually follow through and never miss an opportunity to ask for referrals. The negative side of this referral program is the prospect of feeling the introduction was a bit impersonal.

Here is an overview of a Static Referral System:
1. Ask for referrals from satisfied and happy customers on a consistent basis.
2. Let your customers know about the rewards for your "new" referral system.
3. Make sure your reward system is in place and make it's as generous as

you can, whether that means cash or free services.
4. Create a compelling referral incentive that excites the prospect enough to give your business a try.
5. Follow up immediately with every new referral consistently and systematically. Most businesses start a referral system and then gradually stop following up. This is typically the fault of the business owner.

They become lax and fail to make sure their employees are using the system and following each and every step.

Employees have a tendency to look for shortcuts, and that often has a negative impact on the bottom-line. Always remain vigilant and perform all the steps we're discussing on a daily basis.

The Best Approach for Producing Referrals

Compelling your clients to actively provide you with unlimited and quality referrals is the only way to build a successful referral system. Failing to get referrals is bad for any business, yet receiving a flood of the wrong kind of referrals can be devastating. Unqualified prospects will waste your time, effort, energy and money.

The "art" is in asking for referrals. Believe it or not, you can "train" your clients to ask for referrals.

Your approach needs to be more focused on helping them understand the right way to ask for a referral and the perfect prospect to approach. Five "levers" that can be "pulled" to start the flow of quality referrals.

1- The "Leading question" to ask your clients - with laser-like precision, you can help identify the perfect prospect you're seeking.

2 - Create a referral sheet or "brain tickler" form.

3 - **Get the Address Book** - this requires a direct approach, but ask your clients to access their address book to find five to ten names that suit your demographic profile.

4 - Get to know who your clients know - your client may be new in town and therefore hasn't had time to get to know many people.

5 - Sending a self-mailer on a periodic basis

How to "Time" the Referral Request

Many people cringe when they consider asking for referrals. There is often a fear of rejection, even from regular customers. Fear is something that must be overcome and dismissed if your business is going to thrive.

Just ask!

If you have regular customers, they obviously like you and your business and will more than likely be happy to help you grow your business. Educating your clients on the benefits they and those they refer will receive is a very strong tactic.

This is also the perfect time to give them a thank-you gift, perhaps a free session, lunch on you or whatever freebie is appropriate.

Five major opportunities to "ask" for referrals:
1. When they buy something
2. When you've had a client who has used your services or bought from you numerous times.
3. Asking within a few days of last seeing them
4. Delay asking until you receive praise or a "thank you" from your client
5. Periodically in person or by mail.

Everyone knows at least ten to twenty people, and many often know hundreds. But if they know ten, then those ten also know ten...and so on. Do the math. In a very short time, you could have hundreds of new prospects. And as happy and motivated customers, they should be more than happy to refer you to others, especially when they receive something for their efforts.

Now that you've created your own "Static" referral system, you can take a step up by the implementation of the second tier of a phenomenal referral system.

System # 2 - The Dynamic Referral System

We previously discussed how a Dynamic Referral System can move your Static system to a higher level of performance. You've "recruited" your customers to do a lot of PR for you by promoting your service or business to their friends, associates, and family.

And all you had to do was give them a few perks or free services. The Dynamic Referral System allows you to move the process forward so you can gain access to qualified prospects that would have never heard of you, your business or how you can help them improve their lives.

SIX motivational moves on your part to get your customer "on board":

1. **Simplicity** - how difficult is it to send a "Thank You" card when your regular client sends you a referral? You may feel there's no financial win for you, but the opposite is true…people love to get cards in the mail. They appreciate the human touch. It's worth a few minutes of your time to make your client feel important.

2. **Include A Little Goodie Showing How Much You Appreciate The Referral** - referrals are often a direct result of your excellent service to your client base. Many of them will refer you with no incentive or perks at all.

3. **Allow your client to be the "Big Shot"** - a truly powerful idea would involve giving a select number of your regular clients "coupons" to gift to the people they know inviting them to come to your business and receive a complimentary "whatever."

4. **The "Big Bang" Offer** - once a client has truly impressed you with lots of high-quality referrals, consider offering them a "Big Bang" reward that's tied to what you sell.

5. **Bonuses are GREAT!** - if not the "Big Bang," how about a bonus for each and every new referral they deliver?

6. **Who doesn't like discounts or refunds?** - consider offering refunds or apply the number of refunds to clients who buy from you in the near future…or refund a certain dollar amount if they purchase within a sixty-day time frame when one of their referrals purchases from you.

7. **"Show Me the Money"** - money is generally the most powerful inducement to motivate people to do things for you…but it's the most costly of any of the choices we've mentioned. The actual cost to you is the dollar value of the gift or reward. Think about printing your own "fake" money with a picture of your office or establishment on it…or print something humorous on it and call these pretend dollars "Bucks for Business."

How to Handle "Referrals" from your Clients

We've covered how to recruit and reward your regular customers.

Now we can create a plan for your Referral Prospects.

1. **What special "benefits" can they expect?** - This is your opportunity to share what's so special about you and your business with your potential new customer who came to you as a referral. Share the advantages of doing business with you, how they should expect to be treated as clients or customers and tell them exactly what you will do to encourage their continued patronage.

2. **Will they be treated "special?"** - Put yourself in their place. What would you like to receive from a business like yours? What could you do for them or offer them that would elevate you far above your competition?
3. **Here's the incentive again** - Naturally, you don't have to offer incentives. Your service may be so great and your client satisfaction so huge that you may attract leads from them without any inducement at all.

Preparing Your Client Base

Now that you've created your system and have the model in place for how to respond to, motivate, treat and benefit the referral prospect, what's the process for taking this information and converting the prospect into a paying customer?

By preparing your customers to become YOUR promoters, you will have an army of personal PR representatives on the streets marketing for you. Of course, the easiest and best way to convert a prospect to a customer is by personal communication with you.

Arming your "promoters" with written material they can share with others gives you the opportunity to make sure your message is consistent each time someone else reads your marketing information. A brochure or a few written pages done professionally and created by a printer that contains all the details of your product or service is invaluable.

This is your moment to shine by detailing all the advantages and benefits they'll receive from you and your business along with the ways you differ from your competition.

We've gone over several of the Referral program possibilities and worked over the basic steps for making it work. Let's move forward with the process, shall we?

1. Pick ONE Referral System
2. Put Your Offer and Script Together
3. Test it Yourself and Make Modifications
4. Validate that Your Staff is On Board
5. Implement Monitoring and Tracking Systems

By now, your referral system should be "Dynamic." As you can see, a dynamic referral program can easily double or triple a business's current revenue and profitability. Consider implementing your own immediately and watch your cashflow soar.

Writing a Book

A book is a fast way of creating more leads and sales for your business. Our business has definitely reaped the rewards of book publishing, and we've learned a few secrets of the craft along the way, which we will now divulge to you.

Let's dig deeper into the first secret of book publishing.

Believe it or not, many authors don't actually consider the real reason they are writing their book. It's vitally important to know what outcome you want for your book, especially your first one!

Establish Authority

A book is an instant expert authority booster™ for you and your business, which will position your authority. In your book, you can demonstrate your genius, knowledge, wisdom, and experience.

Get More Sales and Prospects

Published authors make more money and help more people. Becoming an author also allows you to generate multiple income streams.

Books allow you to sell your products and services faster and easier. Books can also talk about what you do, who you do it for, including case studies and results, and invite the reader to try out your products and services.

Before we get into the strategies you can employ in your business, we want to discuss a little shortcut. Everyone has someone in their industry that stands out; someone who seems to be the expert. How did they end up being considered a leader?

Often, it's because of social proof. They have given their peers enough evidence to indicate that they must be an expert.

Whatever business you're in, your #1 priority will always be to get new clients.

But with all these distractions, how do you find the time?

What if we told you that there is a 100% guaranteed way to land new clients, as well as upsell new products, get yourself lucrative speaking gigs, and much more? And what if this solution made you a household name in your field? The go-to expert for advice and information among all your clients, and even the media?

It's more than possible—and you can start right away. The solution is simply to write a book. There can be no better lead generator, foot-in-the-door solution, and media promotional tool. Suddenly, you'll be inundated with new business and become known as the expert in your field. And it's much easier than you might think.

First, let's look in detail at exactly what a book can do for you and your business. Then, later on, we'll describe how easy it is to write such a book.

A book boosts your credibility.

A book, or rather, your book, will position you and your business at the highest level. Think of how much marketing clout you'll have when you can add "#1 best-selling author" to your name, including in business correspondence—right down to your email signature. You can even hand out your book in place of a business card, as well as in meetings. This is a badge of respect that shows you're an authority on the subject of your book and have the experience to back it up.

A book opens doors—literally!

Have you ever had the frustrating experience of not being able to reach the decision-maker in an organisation?

Perhaps you need to meet the CEO of a company you want to do business with, but you are only getting as far as their secretary who always fobs you off. Now imagine sending them your book, gift-wrapped, with a hand-written note to contact you, the book's author.

These people will have already "met" you in your book, so getting in touch with them will be that much easier. In fact, they may very well contact you first.

A book generates leads and builds customer databases.

Believe it or not, a book can be one of the most cost-effective ways of building loyalty and generating new leads and new business. Each sentence, paragraph, and chapter can be a call to action to the reader. It doesn't even need to be a hard sell at this point. You can give away free reports, free trials, free consultations ... the list is almost endless, and it all helps in getting you nearer to closing a deal or winning a new customer.

Do it smartly and you'll capture the reader's email address and other details to add to your database. Consider this also: for every ten books you sell on Amazon, you will likely get contact details for two to four leads, meaning you are getting paid for the sale of the books, and getting qualified leads. What a bargain!

A book can act as a marketing tool for your specific area of expertise.

Your book can include examples of what you or your business does so that readers will understand your business better. These can be in the form of lessons, how-to guides, demonstrations and other hands-on and practical information that will ensure readers are engaged with your business, understand your expertise, and trust that you're the right match for them.

Writing a best-selling book is a way to win professional attention.

If you're a businessperson, you'll know the value of getting speaking gigs and other high-profile jobs, both to establish yourself as a professional and an authority in your field and to promote your products and services. You may even have tried before to get in front of a professional audience to promote yourself or your product, but have been frustrated because the professional body won't take you seriously. So, imagine introducing yourself as the author of a #1 best-selling book and observe the response. In all likelihood, professional organisations and event managers will be queuing up to have you speak at their events.

A book will garner media attention.

Each chapter or section of your book—any part of it, in fact—can be used for promotional purposes in the media. You can send commentators and pundits your book along with your contact details. Inevitably, you'll get invitations to be on talk shows and other media vehicles. Pundits will know what questions to ask you because they've read your book—and you, being the expert that you are, will know how to reply because it's in your book! You can also use chapters, themes and sections of your book to generate social media posts or tweets. You can make these as hands-on as you like, the goal being to keep people aware of you, your book and your business.

Books build local businesses.

A common misconception is that only huge multinational corporations or international companies have books. This simply isn't true. Whether you're a big or small company, global or local, having a best-selling book to your name always puts you ahead of the competition. Imagine handing out copies of your book to potential clients in your local area. This says far more about your professionalism than the photocopied flyers that your closest competitor uses.

Marketing in regulated businesses is easy.

Certain business areas like finance, stocks and share trading, law, and healthcare are heavily-regulated, which puts people off when it comes to writing in these fields.

It shouldn't, because no one can prevent you from writing about personal experiences and from giving personal advice. Just because an industry is regulated doesn't rule you out from writing a book about it.

You will make more money. Simple as that.

Books make people money for all the reasons outlined above. It's all about joining an elite group of people; "a members-only club" who rise above the rest because they've had the confidence and commitment to write one or more books. Your partners will be companies like Amazon and Apple, who will assist you in selling and marketing your book on their own sites or on social media. It's like being on a roller coaster of success that never stops.

But writing a book takes time, and you need to be a professional writer, right?

Wrong. There are actually three myths to debunk here.

Myth #1

The first is believing that you need to be a professional or experienced "author" to write a book. This is one of the biggest hurdles to the practicalities of writing a book. In fact, anyone can write a book, especially a business professional with something to say.

Myth #2

The second is the belief that you have to be super smart to write a book. In fact, most authors are not geniuses—they simply got their hands dirty and set to work writing about what they know. Some will, of course, have used a professional editor to help organize their ideas or tidy up their grammar.

Myth #3

The third is that you have to be rich or famous to write a book, which is plain nonsense. Look at J.K. Rowling, author of the Harry Potter books. When she started out, she was barely making a living. Now she's one of the wealthiest authors alive today.

So, where do you go from here?

At **Evolve Global Publishing**, we have a simple 5-Step system which is designed for small business owners, entrepreneurs, speakers, consultants, coaches and professionals just like you. This will help you to create your book and become recognised as the go-to expert, authority and star in your field. It overcomes the three myths mentioned above that all budding authors have to face.

The system is based on five steps, specifically:

Designing—mainly strategy around your book including the customer journey

Creating—the fast-track method to writing your book

Publishing—the formatting and publish process

Promoting—time to launch your book to the world!

Evolving—what now?

So, How Do You Start?

Our innovative system can take you from scratch to the top-10 best-seller lists in ninety days or less. It's so easy, it's no wonder our client list keeps growing.

And here's why: you don't have to write a single word! In most cases, all we need is ten to fifteen hours of your time to record your content, after which it will then be transcribed to text. Next, you'll work with one of our experienced editors to complete the final version.

You know that you need to write a book. I hope we've convinced you of this fact. Or maybe you're an existing author whose book didn't perform well the first time. This is where we step in. **Evolve Global Publishing** offers packages designed for everyone, from complete beginners to seasoned authors.

Remember: you are an author, not a writer!

Here are some great reasons to write a book ...

Reason #1: Credibility

A book is an instant credibility booster for you and your business.

It supplies you with positioning and authority. In your book, you can demonstrate your genius, knowledge, wisdom, and experience.

Reason #2: Exposure to New Clients

A book is the ultimate foot-in-the-door strategy.

Reason #3: Lead-Generating

You can use your book to get traffic, leads and build your contact database.

A book is a library full of social proof, examples, stories and ways to show you care, that you know what you're talking about, and that you can help the reader to solve just about any challenge.

Reason #4: Showcasing You

Books can be used to sell your services and products faster and easier. They can also talk about what you do, who you do it for, provide case studies and results, and invite the reader to try you out.

Reason #5: Creating New Roles

Books can be used to create new positions for yourself or your client as a consultant.

Reason #6: Speaking Opportunities

Writing books is a great way to get or increase your speaking opportunities.

Reason #7: Media Opportunities and Marketing

Having a book is the perfect way to get media attention, including radio shows, TV interviews, and creating attention on social media. A book can provide a roadmap for your messaging and marketing.

Reason #8: Building Local Business

A book can be used to build your business locally.

Reason #9: Great for Regulated Industries

Regulated industries include fields like financial planning, investing, medical, healthcare, etc. Even though they are regulated, this is not normally a barrier to having a book and can be a great way of marketing in heavily-regulated industries.

Reason #10: Wealth and Wellbeing Accelerant

Published authors make more money and help more people.

If You Can't Automate It You Can't Scale It!

Automation is king. Whenever we consult with any business owner, one of the main focus areas is how automated their sales process, as well as their whole business, is.

Automation isn't just about doing things faster or cutting down on labor; it's also about reducing human error. Human error can easily become a costly liability in both the short-term and long-term. It often means having to repeat processes, wasting time, possibly weakening your relationship with a client, and of course, having to pay someone to repeat the process.

Automation is about doing things better. It's not about finding a shortcut. Humans are best suited not for repetitive tasks, but for creative tasks that require thought and consideration, and that can be completed in several different ways. Machines are best suited to repetitive tasks because they can only do exactly what they're told—assuming they're maintained well, of course.

And for the small business entrepreneur, it's the most valuable tool at your disposal for creating a profitable, efficient, and well-run business that keeps performing without you having to micromanage it. Your time is valuable, and you need to act like it if you want your business to perform. Nobody expects JK Rowling to drive down to the printers and fix their machines. That's not her job.

Just as important as automation, you need to systemize as many processes as you can. This doesn't mean taking staff off work and automating it; it means working with your staff to document their processes so that all of your staff members adhere to a system when completing their tasks. This means consistency; if everyone just does what they think is best, you'll end up with a different result each time, and it's probably not going to be the result you want. You need to create a system for making sales, dealing with customer complaints, and every other crucial aspect of your business that needs to be done *right*.

Look at the key areas of your business and consider what can be done to automate or systemize it.

These are important areas to look at:
- Administration
- Sales
- Marketing
- Customer Services

Here are some areas we have focused on and gotten the most out of over the years:

1. Using Quickbooks to automatically import our bank statements and create templates to learn common transactions. Document the steps in detail so a new person can start quickly in the accounts.
2. Setting up syncs so that once a prospect becomes a customer, we can send their details to our billing system and generate invoices for payment.
3. Implementing a ticket system so we can track and respond to customer issues as well as handle their tasks.
4. Using Zapier to "zap" common tasks that are repetitive. This product is amazing, and digging into some of its features is time well spent. We recently connected Zoom and Vimeo together so that immediately after the call, the video is transferred to Vimeo. Previously we needed to download and upload the files, which took time. Sometimes, we would forget to do it for a call, and it would be a bigger waste of time combing through old calls to find it! With Zapier, you can set it up to sync and forget about it.
5. We use Sanemail to automatically learn our emails and prioritise them based on their importance, and separate types of emails into different folders so that they're easier to manage. When you get thousands of emails a day, it's the only way to keep yourself sane.
6. Streamlining and automating our LinkedIn marketing system, which has brought in well over a million dollars in revenue in the past few years.
7. Implemented an online booking system so the prospect can schedule their own calls. It also activates surveys before the call.
8. Implemented Better Proposals to streamline and allow us to produce proposals quickly and monitor client progress on proposals.

Administration

This area of your business is often undervalued and can be a really great place to start to save money and time.

Hiring an admin assistant is a great idea, but make sure they document all your processes so that your next hire will be able to get up to speed quickly.

Most staff want to fill in the day and don't usually go looking to save time, so you need to implement a culture of looking for these opportunities constantly.

Look at all your tasks in this area and ask yourself: could this be automated or streamlined?

Sales

For your sales area, In most cases, we find there are few systems created for sales. We think the reason why is that most businesses are not created by salespeople. Usually, it's a skilled person striking out on their own. Naturally, these holes appear in their marketing strategies.

For me, there are key numbers you should know in your business:

How much does it cost you to get a "click" from the initial advertisement?

How much does it cost you per lead?

How much does it cost you per sale?

What's your sales conversion rate?

Can you answer all those questions? We don't know of too many business people we have met who can tell us!

Why would you spend money on marketing and not track it!? Generally, the answer is because businesses have no idea how to implement proper systems or processes.

So, try these steps to start with:
- Ask prospects where they heard about you (write it down in a logical place)
- Put out unique offers so you can test specific marketing campaigns
- Create a database of prospects and track the source of business and if they turn into customers
- Make lots of offers and track the results

- Create a campaign worksheet for each time you do a marketing strategy

Simply by tracking and measuring your results, we can guarantee they will improve. What gets watched, monitored, and tracked automatically improves.

Marketing

There is a lot of automation in marketing you can do.

For example, automated campaign emails when someone enquires. Perhaps you could build a Messenger BOT like Manychat to greet customers initially and direct them to the right place.

Social media posts can be automated with RSS feeds, for example.

Customer Services

Almost no one does this! We see a lot of entrepreneurs that start with Gmail and try to run their business off that one email address.

We suggest that, to start with, you should use your own domain name; not a Gmail or Hotmail address.

Gmail signals to your prospects that you are not serious, and that they have no reason to trust you.

Once you have your email in place, create department emails, not people emails.

For example:
- sales@yourdomain
- support@yourdomain
- accounts@yourdomain

We usually create staff emails like: FirstName.LastName@yourdomain

We make it a rule that staff are not to use their email address to communicate directly to the public.

We then assign staff to those departments and ensure that, whenever an email is sent the customer responds back to that department.

This way, you have oversight of the whole business without having to delve into staff personal emails. If a staff member leaves, nothing changes to the outside world and nothing gets missed.

The next step we take is to setup some of these departments to automatically generate a ticket so we can manage the responses and customer service levels.

Some of the ways Evolvepreneur.app was designed to help automate this process include:

Knowledge Base System—so you can document your procedures, as well as customer FAQs all in one secure place based on their security group.

Ticket System—built-in support tickets which can be allocated to different departments. We even auto-create tickets when certain triggers happen on a purchase or survey.

Auto Ticket Emails—we can download emails and create tickets for each request, making it easy to manage customer service requests.

Statistics—we have a comprehensive tracking system that shows all of your web traffic and sources, in addition to a host of other valuable information.

Tagging—allows you to "tag" a user and then automate what happens after that; for example, an email campaign.

Courses & Surveys—create a course and link surveys along the way to test and collect information. This is great for customer projects.

Blogs—connect your RSS feed to your social media posting platform so that every time you write a blog, it automatically distributes it to all your social media profiles.

Staff Training and Systems

An effective Training and Operations Manual will save you and your staff time, energy, and money because you'll be leveraging the power of systems in your business.

The fundamental principle is this:

Every time you do a task without updating your Training and Operations Manual, you can be sure that you'll find yourself doing it again...

Almost everything you do in your business can be systemized and done by other people if you create procedures in your Training and Operations Manual.

Rather than employing more people to get things done, look for ways to systematize what you do to improve consistency and efficiency.

Here are guidelines for creating an Operations and Training Manual in your business…

1. Create a list of tasks being done in your business using the Task Checklist below as a starting point.
2. Then flowchart your business processes so your team can see how all the tasks fit together.
3. Decide which of your tasks to systematize first based on your Time Management Plan. What tasks have you been doing that a lower-paid team member could be doing if it were documented in your Operations and Training Manual? Once you document it and hand it over to a lower-paid team member, you can spend your time on the higher priority tasks.
4. For the tasks being done by other team members, have the team member responsible for each task write down a step-by-step explanation of how they do it.
5. Then, have another person do the task based on the step-by-step explanation and add clarifying steps to the manual as necessary. Have

another person do the task without intervention to make sure the step-by-step explanation is complete enough.
6. Don't overcomplicate systems or people won't follow them. You can use pictures, snapshots of software screens, or videos of people doing the tasks. This will make the systems much easier to follow.
7. Allow the manual to change and grow as time passes on. Make sure your team members keep the Training and Operations Manual current and that everyone knows where it's kept!

Task Checklist

Management Tasks
- Company 1 Page Strategic Plan (vision, mission, values, goals)
- Company organizational chart
- Team member position descriptions, positional contracts, goals, and key performance indicators
- Recruitment system
- Induction program
- Team member training
- Leadership development and career planning
- Conflict resolution
- Contingency staffing plans
- Redundancy systems
- Product Research and Development Tasks
- Developing products, intellectual property
- Developing packaging and collateral material such as catalogs, etc.

Sales and Marketing Tasks
- Create and manage the tactical marketing plan
- Create and manage sales management system
- Designing and producing promotional materials
- Developing leads and prospects
- Creating an advertising plan
- Creating a public relations plan
- Creating a direct mail plan
- Developing and maintaining a database
- Developing and maintaining a website
- Analyzing and tracking sales KPI's
- Continuously measure number and origin of all leads

- Measure conversion rate and average transaction value for each salesperson
- Measure average transaction value for every customer
- Measure profit margins for each product or service

Order Processing and Tracking Tasks
- Taking order and record orders by mail, fax, phone or online
- Fulfilling and packaging the orders
- Confirming details before service or product delivery
- Sending the orders
- Management system for freight, couriers, and vehicles
- Manufacturing and Inventory Tasks
- Maintain order tracking systems
- Selecting vendors
- Maintenance of equipment
- Determining product or service warranties offered
- Establish product or service pricing (retail and wholesale)

Customer Service Tasks
- Responding to customer complaints
- Following up orders
- Measure quality and professionalism of service delivery

Finance, Accounting, Legal Tasks
- Managing the accounting process with daily, weekly, monthly, quarterly and annual reports
- Complete and manage monthly and yearly budgets and forecasts
- Complete weekly income statement
- Complete a monthly balance sheet
- Update daily or weekly cashflow statements
- Managing cash with future borrowing needs secured and available
- Reporting and depositing payroll taxes and withholding payments
- Complete weekly bank reconciliation
- Daily banking activities
- Maintaining an asset register including depreciation

Invoicing and Accounts Receivable Tasks
- Invoicing customers for the orders
- Receiving payments for the orders and crediting customers for payment (cash, check, or credit card)
- Monitoring credit control and age of accounts
- Starting the collection process for outstanding receivables

Accounts Payable Tasks
- Payroll processing
- Purchasing procedures and approvals required
- Payment process for supplies and inventory

Petty cash Corporate Entity Tasks
- Negotiating, drafting and executing contracts
- Developing and protecting intellectual property
- Managing insurance needs and coverage
- Reporting and paying federal, state and other taxes
- Planning for federal, state and other taxes
- Managing and storing records
- Maintaining investor/shareholder relations
- Information flow processes
- Ensuring legal security
- Develop a business plan

Daily Office Physical Space Management Tasks
- Answering the telephone
- Receiving and opening the mail
- Purchasing and maintaining office supplies and equipment
- Answering e-mail
- Dealing with incoming/outgoing delivery needs
- Backing up and archiving data
- Upgrading office equipment
- Appointment Scheduling
- Ensuring physical security
- Staff Resources
- Procedure manual updates

1. Mindset
2. Strategy
3. Implementation
4. **Measure & Review**
5. Pivot & Repeat

What's a KPI?

"If your only tool is a hammer, every problem looks like a nail."

– Abraham Maslow

"Not everything that can be counted counts, and not everything that counts can be counted."

– Albert Einstein

A Key Performance Indicator System (KPIS) is one of the most important strategies you can implement in your business if you want to gain freedom from the operational responsibilities in your company.

A KPIS measures and reports the key activities in your business.

Without KPIs, it's impossible for your team to know how the business is running, how they're doing, and what areas they need to change.

Here's how it works:

Imagine that you have to spend the next few months alone on a tropical island with only your phone. You're allowed to make just one 60-minute call per week to just a few people in your company to direct and coach their activity.

What numbers (usually 5-10) would you like to appear on your phone screen at the end of each day to give you a clear idea of how the day went, how the team performed, and how the business is running?

What numbers will give you the basis for coaching your team to run the business effectively while you are away?

Here's a sample list of common KPIs used by most successful entrepreneurs.

- Clicks to Website Lead Signup rate from Landing Page
- Leads generated
- Lead Conversion rate
- Cost per lead
- Cost per click
- Inbound calls
- Revenue per customer
- Quotes given
- Appointments set
- Quote to Sale Conversion
- New sales closedAverage sale value
- Revenue generated
- Revenue growth rate
- Gross profit per unit sold
- Average transaction value
- Billable hours per employee
- Average hourly rate
- Customer satisfaction rate
- Customer retention rate
- Customer Complaints
- Gross Profit Margin
- Net Profit Margin
- Advertising to Sales
- Payroll to Sales
- Return on Equity

Questions to consider as you're crafting your KPI system:

How often do you want to review your KPIs? (Daily, weekly)

What key positions and responsibilities do you want to measure? (review your org chart and job descriptions)

What KPIs are most important to you? (Numbers, ratios, percentages)

How do you want the information delivered? (Email, Spreadsheet, Cloud Solution)

How will you communicate the KPIs to your team? (Email, Dashboard)

4 Measure & Review

What indicates good performance in this position?

What are the big picture goals?

How do I measure good performance?

Tracking and Monitoring Your Results

Would you like to double your marketing results without spending any money?

Tracking your results is very important. Too often, we spend hours on the design of an advertising project and forget to find out if it worked. Your gut feeling often doesn't tell you the full story.

What happens when you track your advertising is that you pay attention to what works and what doesn't.

Future campaigns are only placed based on what works, and you tend to focus on one or two key methods that work instead of throwing money at all of them.

What you are looking for is a couple of key indicators, create a front sheet for each campaign you have and place the details with it. This means you have a resource folder for future campaigns and purely doing this step will increase your results…

Advertising Project Name: _____

Cost of advertising: $ _____

Number of Leads Generated _____

Cost per Lead: $ _____

Number of Sales _____

Cost per Sale $ _____

Gross Profit per Sale $ _____

Return on investment % _____

For example, if a Facebook Ad cost you $500, and you had 10 leads and 1 sale, and your gross profit per sale is $1000:

Cost per lead	$ 50
Cost per sale	$ 500
Return on investment	200%

This is not bad, considering the banks pay less than 3% Interest in most countries!

If you factor in the lifetime value of this new customer based on the previous result, if you spend $500, you will make $3,000 over 5 years.

I'll leave it up to the accountants to work out the return of $3,000 on a $500 investment.

The bottom line is that marketing and advertising are the best-paid work you will ever get. That's why many small businesses fail—they don't understand that, without a steady supply of new business and looking after your existing customers, their shelf life is about 5 years (tops!).

From here, you can work out where the majority of your business comes from and what it costs. In our experience, the cheapest advertising yields the best results.

1 Mindset

2 Strategy

3 Implementation

4 Measure & Review

5 Pivot & Repeat

Creating Your Strategic Plan

When we consult with a new client, we usually ask them some key questions about their strategic plans.

More often than not, there aren't a lot of detailed strategies that business owners can articulate.

But without a strategy, their tactics will fail.

We have a process we use to create a one-page strategic plan on one large sheet of paper.

While we can't show you the whole plan, we can give you some of the key components.

1. **Your Dreams** - Most people don't have visions; they have dreams. Consider these seven questions relating to your dream – Who, What, When, Where, How, Why, as well as "but Should we or Shouldn't we?"

If you can get your decisions correct, your life will start to fall into place much easier.

2. **S.W.O.T:** What are the top 3- 5 items for each?
   - Strengths
   - Weaknesses
   - Threats
   - Opportunities

3. **What are your core values?** Things you should or shouldn't do – list your core values then relate stories from the past 3-12 months that represent each core value.

4. **What's you Core Purposes and Big Hairy Goal?** List your core purpose and your Big Hairy Goal. Write down what you're doing to reach both. Create clear 90-day actions.

The core purpose revolves around a single word or image and comes out of the impetus for why the founder(s) launched the company—*The Big Hairy Goal*–which is likely to be ten years away. Then align with your business fundamentals and with the core purpose. Microsoft's BHAG for the 1990s was to have "a computer on every desk and in every home."

Then create specific "to do's" in the next 90 days to live your core values, core purpose, and BIG Goal.

5. **Revenues & Profits** - Pick a comfortable point three to five years from now to determine desired Revenues and Profit.

6. **What's your brand promise?** – You will need to list your three Brand Promises – these are three ways you both relate to your customers but also make you different from the competition.

7. **What are the small priorities** for the next three to five years necessary to reach your outcome targets (Revenue, Profit, Market Share)?

8. **Set an annual budget** - Create a set of measurable outcomes.

9. **What are your critical numbers?** - This is a critical decision you make coming out of the strategic planning process.

10. **What are the three to five priorities** for the next year that support the Critical Numbers and what you want your annual outcomes while making progress on your longer-term targets?

11. **Every 90 Days, Set a 90-Day Budget** and fill in like you did the annual column.

I hope this helps with your strategic planning process.

Why Failure is Important

Let's talk about failure.

We think it's crazy that children are taught at school only to succeed—for example, they are given exams, and if they fail, they get held back.

By doing this, schools are teaching children that failure is bad, and they end up punishing themselves mentally for it. They set out to avoid failure and become risk-adverse.

Perhaps this is why so many entrepreneurs did badly at school

It's true—school isn't designed to prepare you for the real world. But perhaps it's worthwhile trying to figure out why.

Of course, you need to pass tests and assignments to prove that you're learning and keeping up with the class.

But why not also allow students to fail and teach them how to cope with it in a safe environment?

As well, if you needed brain surgery, you would probably prefer to get the smartest surgeon; the one who was top of the class.

But entrepreneurship isn't about success. That follows if you get it right, but along the way, you learn so much more from failure.

Fear of failure can cripple an entrepreneur from taking the risks they need to succeed.

Failure is simply a lesson on what not to do the next time. Sometimes, failure actually turns into a massive success.

For example, antibiotics were invented from a failed experiment by Professor Alexander Fleming when he noticed mould from an experiment after cleaning up. Where would we be today without that discovery?

You want to fail fast, try things if they don't work, then review why, and move on. Don't dwell on the failure; ask better questions about what happened and why. It's most likely that you will suffer far more failures than success in your career. The old saying, "it takes 20 years to become an overnight success" is very true.

In fact, it's probably why many older people have become successful beyond their 50s or 60s, like the inventor of KFC.

So, you want to fail in an educated way. This doesn't mean taking unreasonable, expensive risks. Take small steps toward your goals and fail in small ways to start with.

In many sports, they teach athletes how to fall and not hurt themselves. This is what you want to do—fail, but don't fail so badly that you lose everything in the process.

The bad news, however, is that sometimes dramatic and massive failure can also lead to huge success.

Having lost millions of dollars in failed business over the years, it can be hard to look back and wonder if there was a better way that just wasn't evident at the time.

A great saying I recently heard was, "You're not dead yet." This means you can always get up again and keep moving!

So, start by flexing your failure muscle with small disasters, and as you get better at it, upgrade to bigger ones.

Expanding Through Advertising

An area that many entrepreneurs get stuck on is the advertising of their offers. Often, they overspend with rose-coloured glasses when presented with a promotional idea. You need to consider the risk vs reward when looking at any advertising spend. Few advertising companies guarantee results, so start small and test rollout only when you start to see viable results.

Below are some ideas for getting the right mindset for advertising campaigns.

Customer Life Time Value

Customer lifetime value is one of the most important things to ask yourself. It is, in effect, how much you are prepared to pay to attract a new customer. This is a fundamental lever for advertising.

The basic formula is:

A = What is the typical gross profit per sale to this customer

B = How long will this customer remain a customer

C = How much profit per year from this customer

A + B X C = $$$$

For example, if you make $1,000 profit out of the first sale and expect to make around $500 per annum profit for 5 years, then the lifetime value is $3,000.

So, in effect, you could spend up to $3,000 to get this customer (and keep him) and still break even.

It is vital to know roughly what each customer is worth to your business over time. This forms the basis of your advertising budget, as well as your income potential in the future. Often, the costs outweigh the profit in winning a new customer when you factor in your time. Ongoing revenue from this client will make up the difference.

Advertising 101

The power of words is a force you should never trivialize. The more your target audience sees your company name in association with a product or service of considerable worth, the more likely they will patronize your business.

Advertising is one facet of a comprehensive marketing campaign. It provides a direct line to your customers and prospective customers regarding your product or service.

Your goals can change as your business evolves:

The Start-up/Pioneering Stage – you are new in the marketplace. You need to advertise heavily to command your prospect's attention.

The Competitive Stage – once you have built your identity and grabbed your prospect's attention, you have a crowded marketplace and you need to stress the differences between you and your competitors.

The Sustaining Stage – remind prospects you are still in business with lighter levels of continuous or seasonal advertising campaigns.

Good advertising engenders action and persuades the prospective customer to try your product or service.

When developing your advertising campaign, focus on these things:

Market Definition – determine who your most productive audience will be in order to make your advertising more effective.

Budgeting – create a budget based on what you can afford to spend and upon the media where you will get the best results.

Media Planning – gather facts on your advertising media under consideration and determine the best ones to reach your prospective customers.

Creative Strategy – choose the most effective message and visuals to use in your advertising campaign.

Types of Advertising Vehicles
- Social Media (organic)
- Banner Advertising
- Pay per Click Advertising
- Television (cheaper than you think in regional areas)

- Radio (can be cost-effective in some situations)
- Newspapers
- Magazines
- Outdoor Billboards
- Public Transport
- Direct Mail (including postcards and flyers)
- Newsletters (including your own)
- Websites (including your own)
- Other media, such as brochures, handouts and business cards/magnets

The Creative Campaign

There are seven basic characteristics all creative messages should have:

1. They are simple and easily understood
2. They are truthful
3. They are informative
4. They are sincere
5. They are customer-oriented
6. They tell who, what, where, when, why and how.
7. Of course, most important of all, they sell benefits…benefits…benefits!

Designing the campaign and promotional material

There are several steps you should take when designing a campaign.

Create a sense of immediacy – response diminishes over time, you need to get your reader to respond now, act today!

Repetition sells – keep weaving and re-weaving the same sales pitch throughout the ad. The more times someone hears or reads something, the more believable it becomes. You were taught at school to avoid writing repetitiously, but when writing copy, forget about this rule and repeat, repeat, and repeat!

Hit the buttons – different people will be drawn in by different things. One person may want quality; another might like the simplicity of a product. Decide what is different and exciting about your product and tell your audience how and why they need to have what you sell.

Sell the sizzle, not the sausage – It's an old one but a good one! Sell the benefits of doing business with you, not the product. Use plain, simple English.

Evaluate other ads – collect all kinds of ads and study them.

Some Visual tips

   Start with a headline; headlines make ads work. Ego puts your name at the top of the ad!

   A mix of upper and lowercase letters are easier to understand; use all caps sparingly
- Photographs work better than illustrations
- Small print captions under pictures are well-read
- Set long text justified i.e lined up flush left and right
- Don't crowd your advertisement with different typefaces
- Consider reverse advertising which is white on black. Use in a limited environment as too much can make your advertisement hard to read
- Consider colour or spot colour advertising
- Decide on whether you want a border or not.
- If your advertisement looks more like an editorial, try to get it printed without one.

Some do's and don'ts
- Never, ever, misspell any words in your advertising copy. This is suicide.
- Don't make claims that you can't follow through.
- Make sure all contact information is correct.
- Use a readable type size.
- Make your ads look as professional as possible..
- Use testimonials when necessary to highlight the success of your product or service.
- Highlight specific benefits – don't waste space on vague, generalized statements indicating why your company is "the best".

Advertising Workshop
1. List some different benefits of your product or service that will entice people to buy.
2. How are you going to create a sense of immediacy?
3. What is your main repetitive message?
4. What results do you expect from your advertising?

5 Pivot & Repeat

Advertising on a shoestring?

There you go - I bet I caught your attention with this headline.

You'd probably like to spend thousands of dollars on advertising, but the reality is, you can't. In fact, having a big advertising budget can often be worse than having a small one.

Here are some ideas to get the best "bang for your buck":

Strategic Partnerships – team up with non-competing businesses in your area and offer a combined service. Target your market, right down to the headline.

Consistent image – make sure all your marketing and internal correspondence match up. Business cards, letterhead, fax headers, etc. All with the same layout and message.

Business Cards – the most under-utilized piece of cardboard. Always have your cards with you and use them as an excuse to get your prospect's card. I've lost count the number of times I have asked someone for their business card and they fumble around and manage to give me one (not two – one for my friend!) OR say "we've run out"! The main aim of your card is to give it out, so don't worry about the cost; they are costing you more in your wallet in lost business. Make your cards interesting. It's not enough to just have your name, rank and serial number. It's a tiny display ad; treat it that way.

Don't reinvent the wheel – if you see a successful campaign, copy it and try to adapt it for your business.

The Internet – create a website, or better still, sales funnels, and make sure you have your own domain name. Make sure your email address is your business name, not Gmail or Hotmail. This shows prospects you are small and on the cheap.

Be Visible – be a visible member of the offline or online community. They'll remember you were there personally much longer than any display advertisement.

Referrals – create a referral program. Satisfied customers are your best advertisements. Provide them with some incentive to refer their friends and colleagues. Make sure you thank them when they send you business; a nice letter and maybe a movie ticket or a gift card. A great idea we saw recently was to give someone a $500 Star Bucks Gift card. This means every time they buy a coffee they will remember you - and $500 goes a long way!

Coupons – used carefully, coupons can be a good source of business.

Sponsorship – sponsor something worthwhile; sports teams, charities, and community organizations. Often the cost is nominal in comparison to a promotional activity.

The Future of Social Media

What is the future of social media platforms?

Well, we really have no idea!

But let's think about history and make some educated guesses.

The rise of Big Tech and the detailed tracking of humans over the past 15 years has started to backfire on these corporations. In the documentary Social Dilemma, they say that the only 2 products that refer to their customers as "users" are software and drugs.

The "users" are starting to wake up. The current generation of kids refer to Facebook as a platform for old people. There are always new platforms emerging and many of them are talking about the protection of privacy.

It's entirely possible that people might move to a subscription-based social media experience, sort of like a Netflix for Facebook.

LinkedIn already does offer upgrades for a deeper use of their platform, for example. After all, your data is valuable, and what you might do in the future is even more valuable to an advertiser.

Perhaps in the coming years, there will be an AA for social media where people have to learn how to get off the platforms.

To respond to growing anger, these platforms are likely to go through many changes and may very well hurt the entrepreneurs who rely on it for the survival of their business.

In this ever-changing landscape lies massive opportunity.

The reality is that these platforms come and go just like governments do. Does the name "MySpace" ring a bell?

But these new corporations have massive wealth behind them. They can jump into other investment options. Like Google with self-driving cars, Amazon with their space program, and Facebook with virtual reality.

So, let's not try to predict the future; rather, let's design our own.

Many of these platforms have attracted young entrepreneurs especially by allowing them to not have to worry about building and managing a website. There is a cafe down the road from us that only has a Facebook page, and that's the extent of their online presence.

The danger here is that, if they get too many bad reviews, they could easily end up being banned or locked out.

What you want to focus on is creating a platform where you can attract prospective customers and keep them on your website, not being distracted by the latest shiny object on their social media feed.

If you have their email address, you have the one thing that these platforms never want to give you and now you can probably see why!

With Evolvepreneur.app, we have the ability to create multiple front-end websites that all lead to a back-end community site that also helps your customer track their downloads, orders, and engage in your educational and marketing materials.

At the same time, you can start a podcast or on-demand show that your prospects and customers can subscribe to and get alerted when new content comes out.

Make sure you own your own stuff and tread your own path. Use social media as a tool, not a platform.

WRAPPING UP

Did you enjoy this book?

If you enjoyed this book, we would really appreciate a 5-star review on the platform you bought this book from.

You can also find other ways to buy this book at: *https://evolvepreneur.club/show-book/B088K64W7R*

If you didn't like our book, email us at *info@evolvepreneur.club* and let's see if we can help!

Make sure you join our free community at *www.evolvepreneur.club*

Where To From Here?

This book was created by Evolvepreneur as a grand design to help you create, grow and dominate your market.

Your journey is yet to begin until you start to implement the ideas in this book. After all, implementation and action-taking are the real keys to success.

Evolvepreneur offers many ways for you to get involved and even interact with like-minded individuals and we look forward to hearing from you and especially your wins.

Here are a few ways to connect with us:
- Join our free Facebook Group
- Listen to our Podcasts
- Join as a regular or mastermind member
- Become an expert and help our community

All of this can be found at www.evolvepreneur.club and we are waiting right now...

Working with John North

John North is a Seven-Time #1 International Best Selling Author who is regarded as a versatile and experienced entrepreneur with a solid background in Accounting, Banking, Business Management, Finance, Personal Development, IT, Software and Strategic Marketing.

John has written six #1 Best Selling Books about book publishing, business strategy and internet marketing, and a book about Squash.

John is the CEO of Evolve Systems Group. He is a serial entrepreneur who has created many products and services that are designed to empower business owners and entrepreneurs. Some of these ventures include: Evolve Global Publishing, Evolvepreneur.app, Evolvepreneur.club, EvolveYourBusiness, and Evolve Mobile.

John is passionate about helping business owners become smarter and more strategic about their marketing efforts. He constantly pushes the envelope of what's possible in this modern era and is widely regarded among his peers as very innovative and highly creative in his approach.

Evolve Global Publishing is a premium service that John created to enable him to help thousands rather than hundreds of entrepreneurs. He believes that anyone can follow a system to success, but the missing keys are implementation and accountability.

The Evolve Global Publishing platform and its methodologies allow an entrepreneur and potential author to create and publish their own book in a little as 90 days without writing a single word! His latest venture, Evolvepreneur.app, is an all-in-one platform designed to allow entrepreneurs to take control of their future by being less reliant on using social media for managing their business online.

If you would like to work with him personally, reach out to John via his website www.johnnorth.com.au and book a no-obligation chat.

About Evolve Global Publishing

Evolve Global Publishing has been responsible for publishing hundreds of books, and all of them, without fail, have achieved #1 best-seller status on Amazon.

Evolve Global Publishing offers a worry-free professional service to achieve the creation, publishing, and launch of your book.

We are about to introduce you to the "Single Most Powerful Tool to Promote and Market Your Business":

- The solution is 564 years old.
- It's not high-tech.
- It's won the hearts and minds of people all over the world.
- It can create wealth and fame for those who understand its power.
- It works in any business or industry, in any language, anywhere in the world.

Published authors make more money, get more attention, have more freedom, and are given the opportunity to share their message with the world.

Research has also shown that entrepreneurs who have written books have a distinct advantage. According to a BusinessWeek survey, 96% of authors saw positive benefits from their book, such as easier access to media/PR exposure, the command of higher speaking and consulting fees, an increase in their credibility and reach—and simply more income.

Imagine…

You can create a nonfiction book and become a bestseller while attracting a steady flow of new business.

You're connected to the biggest names in your industry, capitalising on your star power to promote your products and services.

You create a growing tribe on Facebook, LinkedIn, YouTube, Google+, and iTunes, and receive lots of new business from all of this exposure.

You become recognized as an authority—even a celebrity in your field—in a few months, not years or decades.

You attract people who want to join you and help you and your business, life, and mission because your vision inspires and moves them to action.

The biggest brands, platforms, and networks in the world, like Google, YouTube, Amazon, Twitter, Apple, Instagram, LinkedIn, Facebook, etc., will help promote and sell your books, build your list and reputation, all while promoting your content to social networks.

Evolve Global Publishing's normal publishing process includes:
- Creation of your content either from your existing assets or through a series of recorded interviews
- Book cover and title—creation/design or use your existing files
- Formatting of your manuscript for print and digital formats, including softcover and hardcover
- Number one best-seller campaign in multiple categories
- Publishing for digital and print for Amazon, CreateSpace, Apple, and Kobo
- Arrangement of physical printed books (additional print cost)
- Optional editing and proofreading services

Publishing Solutions

Once your book is ready for worldwide release, Evolve Global Publishing will enable your book to be purchased on virtually every known platform. We will make your book available to thousands of major online and offline bookstores and retailers, which expands the size of the potential audience for your books.

#1 International Best-Seller Campaign

As part of your membership package, we will execute our #1 international best-seller strategy designed to have you listed as, at the least, #1 best-seller, with a goal for #1 in three Amazon categories in four countries (one per country).

We will continue to promote your book until we achieve this goal. Because achieving #1 best-seller status requires significant marketing and promotion on our side, we charge an additional fee.

Wrapping Up

Get it All Done in as Little as 90 Days

Our goal is to assist you to create your content and publish it within a 90-day period. However, these timescales can vary depending on individual requirements. But it's about getting you out there fast! The ones that invest in this system will change their lives and businesses forever.

The question is—are you simply interested? Or are you committed?

Are you committed to getting the additional freedom a book will give you, being in an elite group of published authors, and getting recognized and standing out?

We look forward to making you our next best-selling author!

Book an obligation-free call at *www.evolveglobalpublishing.com*, and let's get you started!

About Evolve Your Business

Business Owners, Entrepreneurs, and Ideapreneurs

Our most intensive and feature-rich coaching and consulting program designed for high-performing entrepreneurs and focused on major performance improvements in their operations.

Our consultants will demand the highest levels of performance from you and your team. If you are looking to expand your operations, launch new products, transition leadership, or move towards franchising, then this is the program for you.

Whilst we believe that we can help every business, we also know that there a lot of factors that ensure our client's success.

For that reason, we offer a free no-obligation Business Analysis.

We apply numerous marketing strategies in order to spread your brand on the World Wide Web. From video marketing to podcasting, search engine optimization to lead generation, and different techniques to promote through social media, we know all there is to give your company the boost it needs to pull ahead of your rivals. Rest assured that you cannot go wrong with our marketing strategy.

Find out more at *www.EvolveYourBusiness.co*

About Evolvepreneur.app

Coaches, Consultants, Authors, Podcasters, Publishers, and Mastermind Groups

Discover The New Revolution in Community-Based eLearning and Marketing Solutions...

- Course Creation,
- Success Journeys,
- Goals,
- Progress-Based Learning,
- eCommerce,
- Affiliate & Membership Management,
- Social Community Networking & Learning,
- Customer Support Module,
- Contact Management,
- Gamification,
- eMail Marketing,
- Podcasting,
- Blogs,
- Survey & Quizzes tightly integrated with Courses Blogs & Podcasts,
- Messaging,
- Coach Directory Mastermind & Coaching Modules

The Evolvepreneur APP Platform combines social networking and community-based learning to unleash an incredible opportunity to launch, scale, and grow your business exponentially, right now...TODAY!'

For more information, check out *www.evolvepreneur.app*

Admin Dashboard
Notifications
Support Tickets
My Zone
Users
CRM
Marketing
Blog
Podcasts
E-Commerce
E-learning
Surveys & Forms
Project Manager
Website Manager
Manage Media
Knowledge Base
Gamification
Amazon Settings
On Demand Shows
Admin Settings
458
Orders
777
User Registrations
114
Blog Posts
40
Courses
Visits Overview
1562 Visits
1223 Unique Visits
0h 03m 39s Average Visit Duration
4 actions (page views, downloads, outlinks etc.) per visit
61% Bounce Rate
See All Stats
Support Tickets
9
19
387
406
Stats
Visitor Map
575 visits
Affiliates
46
Orders
43
Orders Paid
12
Active Affiliates
Social Networks

About Evolvepreneur.club

Welcome to the Ultimate Learning and Social Site for Online Entrepreneurs!

Join Our Community (For Free)

Evolvepreneur.club is a community-based learning portal for everything about online business and marketing:

- Interact with like-minded individuals
- We can help you find the right tools and resources for the job
- Comprehensive Bookstore
- Certified Outsourcers and Coaches Directory
- Podcast
- Knowledge Base

Join today for free at **www.evolvepreneur.club**

OTHER BOOKS

AUTHORITY

Strategic Concepts from 15 International Thought Leaders to Create Influence, Credibility and a Competitive Edge for You and Your Business

In this book, you will find the collective wisdom of 15 international thought leaders, scattered across three continents and multiple industries, as they share their best strategies for building influence and authority.

Covering everything from video and print media to social media and consulting, Authority lets you inside the minds of experts who have built their own authority and helped countless others do the same. Whether you find yourself in a small business or large, virtual or traditional, you can benefit from the increased impact and success that comes with Authority.

Contributors:
- JOHN NORTH
- CHRISTINE ROBINSON
- MATT SMITH
- ADAM JOHNSON
- LARRY MORRISON
- CATHY FYOCK
- ALLAN MCLENNAN
- JENN FOSTER
- DENISE GABEL
- JASON B.A. VAN CAMP
- MARK LEONARD
- MELANIE JOHNSON
- NATHAN JOHNSON
- EVERETT O'KEEFE
- GEORGE SMOLINKSI

Everything You Know About Marketing Is Wrong!

#1 Bestseller

By JOHN NORTH

How to Immediately Generate More Leads, Attract More Clients and Make More Money

In this #1 Best Selling Book, we'll reveal the strategies you can immediately deploy that will enable you to out-think, out-market and out-sell your competition.

What we want to do in this book is to teach you a system for marketing your business... to a point where it becomes instantly obvious to your prospects that they would be an idiot to do business with anyone other than you... at any time, anywhere or at any price.

What most business owners will focus on is generating more leads at any cost but this isn't the best way to attract prospects to your business.

We can help you build a million-dollar or even multi-million-dollar business. Also, make sure you take advantage of the free bonuses in the book!

OTHER BOOKS

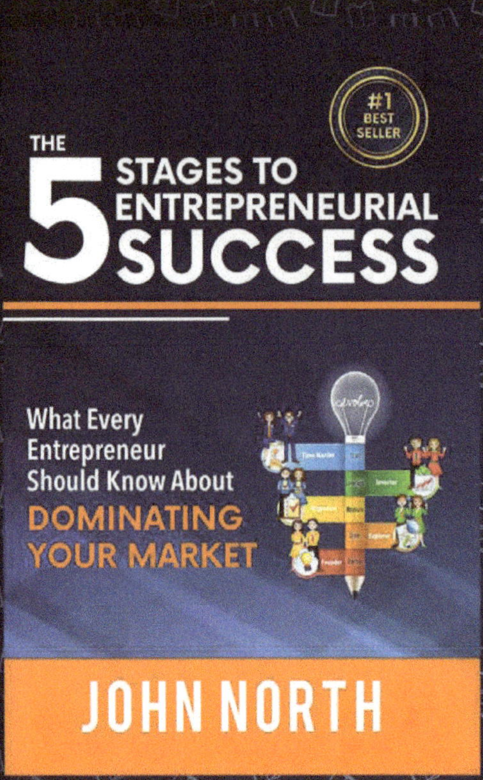

The 5 Stages To Entrepreneurial Success:

It's a common question, but what makes a successful entrepreneur?

It's my belief that success isn't just about making money. Most people start a business for the freedom they expect it to give them. The cold hard reality is that most entrepreneurs end up working longer hours and for a lot less than a typical wage for an average job.

Entrepreneurs commit to "the hustle" because they have a much bigger vision for their future than the average person. But then, if they work harder than an average worker, then why doesn't every entrepreneur become massively successful?

The fact is, many entrepreneurs are making the same mistakes year after year. Learn what those are and how to avoid them in **The 5 Stages To Entrepreneurial Success.**

Book Publishing Secrets For Entrepreneurs

Having a published book is one of the most powerful ways to gain authority in your industry.

It's the ultimate marketing strategy that sells itself. Discover how to write and publish your own book and get it into the hands of as many people as possible. Learn how to create a book around your business, or even launch a whole new business.

The great thing about writing a book is that it not only ensures that you get crystal clear on what you do, but also how you do it. The five steps that guided the creation of this book will save countless hours of your time.

Create it, conceive it, and publish it - all in less than 90 days. Then, evolve your completed book and become a #1 International Best Selling Author!

OTHER BOOKS

Internet Marketing Secrets

WHAT MOST BUSINESS OWNERS DON'T KNOW... AND WILL NEVER KNOW... ABOUT INTERNET MARKETING

#1 INTERNATIONAL BESTSELLER

Discover many low or no-cost Internet lead generation tactics that you can begin using today to double your marketing results immediately

JOHN NORTH

"For any business to succeed in the current era using internet marketing isn't an option any longer, it's an absolute must!"

The purpose of this book is to educate and encourage business owners and managers on the main aspects of internet marketing so that they can learn and apply the key principles along with traditional marketing techniques to literally leapfrog competitors whilst generating substantially more sales, profits, and cash.

Internet marketing has now become a necessity as part of your marketing strategies. Without internet marketing, it's highly unlikely your company can increase sales or revenue.

Discover many low- or no-cost internet lead generation tactics that you can begin using today to double your marketing results immediately.

https://evolvepreneur.club/show-book/B00MMI4Y96

The Game of Squash

#1 INTERNATIONAL BESTSELLER

The Game of SQUASH
5 Easy Ways to Improve Your Game And Win More Matches

JAMES ETHAN & JOHN NORTH

The Game of Squash is written to help beginners to advanced players get more out of their game and find ways to win more matches. We believe squash can become very addictive, but what a wonderful addiction!

Most players strive to improve, but lack of discipline or knowledge can hold you back. **The Game of Squash** is designed to give you an easy resource for all things squash.

Here are just some of the topics we cover:

• Who can play squash–a description of the game and what you can expect to get out of it

• A basic understanding of the rules

• How to choose the best squash racket for you

• Tips and tricks for improving your game

https://evolvepreneur.club/show-book/B018JXYRF4

Lightning Source UK Ltd.
Milton Keynes UK
UKHW050204100822
407064UK00001B/3

9 781637 520765